Trust: A Very Short Introduction

Titles in the series include the following:

AFRICAN HISTORY John Parker and
   Richard Rathbone
AGEING Nancy A. Pachana
AGNOSTICISM Robin Le Poidevin
AGRICULTURE Paul Brassley and
   Richard Soffe
ALEXANDER THE GREAT
   Hugh Bowden
ALGEBRA Peter M. Higgins
AMERICAN HISTORY Paul S. Boyer
AMERICAN IMMIGRATION
   David A. Gerber
AMERICAN LEGAL HISTORY
   G. Edward White
AMERICAN POLITICAL
   HISTORY Donald Critchlow
AMERICAN POLITICAL PARTIES
   AND ELECTIONS L. Sandy Maisel
AMERICAN POLITICS
   Richard M. Valelly
THE AMERICAN PRESIDENCY
   Charles O. Jones
AMERICAN SLAVERY
   Heather Andrea Williams
THE AMERICAN WEST Stephen Aron
AMERICAN WOMEN'S HISTORY
   Susan Ware
ANAESTHESIA Aidan O'Donnell
ANARCHISM Colin Ward
ANCIENT EGYPT Ian Shaw
ANCIENT GREECE Paul Cartledge
THE ANCIENT NEAR EAST
   Amanda H. Podany
ANCIENT PHILOSOPHY Julia Annas

ANCIENT WARFARE Harry Sidebottom
ANGLICANISM Mark Chapman
THE ANGLO-SAXON AGE John Blair
ANIMAL BEHAVIOUR
   Tristram D. Wyatt
ANIMAL RIGHTS David DeGrazia
ANXIETY Daniel Freeman and
   Jason Freeman
ARCHAEOLOGY Paul Bahn
ARISTOTLE Jonathan Barnes
ART HISTORY Dana Arnold
ART THEORY Cynthia Freeland
ASTROPHYSICS James Binney
ATHEISM Julian Baggini
THE ATMOSPHERE Paul I. Palmer
AUGUSTINE Henry Chadwick
THE AZTECS David Carrasco
BABYLONIA Trevor Bryce
BACTERIA Sebastian G. B. Amyes
BANKING John Goddard and
   John O. S. Wilson
BARTHES Jonathan Culler
BEAUTY Roger Scruton
THE BIBLE John Riches
BLACK HOLES Katherine Blundell
BLOOD Chris Cooper
THE BODY Chris Shilling
THE BOOK OF MORMON
   Terryl Givens
BORDERS Alexander C. Diener and
   Joshua Hagen
THE BRAIN Michael O'Shea
THE BRICS Andrew F. Cooper
BRITISH POLITICS Anthony Wright

Katherine Hawley

TRUST

A Very Short Introduction

OXFORD
UNIVERSITY PRESS

OXFORD
UNIVERSITY PRESS

Great Clarendon Street, Oxford, ox2 6DP,
United Kingdom

Oxford University Press is a department of the University of Oxford.
It furthers the University's objective of excellence in research, scholarship,
and education by publishing worldwide. Oxford is a registered trade mark of
Oxford University Press in the UK and in certain other countries

First Edition published in 2012

Impression: 9

British Library Cataloguing in Publication Data

Data available

Library of Congress Cataloging in Publication Data

Data available

ISBN 978-0-19-969734-2

Printed and bound by
CPI Group (UK) Ltd, Croydon, CR0 4YY

To Fiona and Daniel, since I promised

Contents

Acknowledgements

I have had interesting conversations about trust with all sorts of helpful people, but in particular I would like to thank those who introduced me to ideas beyond my disciplinary comfort zone, including Amber Carpenter, Cathy Crockford, Jon Hesk, Martin Kusch, Jennifer Nagel, Jennifer Saul, and, long ago, Simon Schaffer.

List of illustrations

Introduction
Trust and distrust at the breakfast table

I woke up this morning to broadcaster John Humphrys telling me it was 7 o'clock on Thursday 26th August, then listened to the latest news from Pakistan, hoping my recent donation to the flood appeal had made some small difference. My husband brought me coffee made with grounds labelled 'Fairtrade' from the local supermarket, milk he'd picked up from the doorstep, and water from the tap. I told him I'd take the kids to school, and he set off for work, driving through the rush-hour traffic to catch the train. The children and I ate our cereal – not too sugary, for the sake of their health – and I sent them upstairs to get dressed. After I'd put dinner money in their bags, we walked up the road to cross with the lollipop lady, and the kids ran into school. I bought a newspaper on the way home, unlocked the front door, then picked up a few early birthday cards from the doormat.

Without trust, we would have been paralysed by inaction. I trusted my husband to make a decent cup of coffee, and to drive carefully on his way to the office he says he works in. He trusted me to take care of our kids, and drop them at school as I'd promised. The kids took it from me that it was a school day, and that I hadn't sneaked yucky raisins into their breakfast.

We trust acquaintances – from the unseen milkman to the schoolteachers to John Humphrys (we like to consider him almost a friend). And we trust complete strangers – motorists, the BBC's correspondent in Pakistan, workers at the water treatment plant, government nutritionists. We trust institutions – the BBC, Oxfam, the local school, the supermarket and its Fairtrade certification, the Royal Mail, the currency system. And how can I be sure tomorrow is really my birthday? I didn't check the calendar when I emerged mewling and puking.

Trust is essential – we just can't do everything for ourselves, or check the evidence for everything we believe. We must trust if we are to get what we want, but we must also trust when we're trying to help others, whether that's our own children or disaster victims far away. Patterns of trust may differ between modern technological societies and traditional close-knit communities, but trust is crucial in both contexts.

Yet we wouldn't get far without a healthy dose of distrust too. I buy Fairtrade coffee (at least, I think I do) because I distrust the big producers' claims to treat their workers decently. I lock the door when I go out, and I don't leave the kids to select their own chocolatey breakfast; I'm not sure whether I can trust them to get dressed without my nagging. If I trusted my husband to refuel the car, I'd run the risk of getting stranded. And while I trust the teachers to educate and care for the kids, I don't trust them to provide the perspective on religion I'd like. (But don't tell the school I said so: I don't trust them to react calmly.)

We owe it to ourselves and others to get it right about trust.

Chapter 1
What are trust and distrust?

Trust is at the centre of a whole web of concepts: reliability, predictability, expectation, cooperation, goodwill, and – on the dark side – distrust, insincerity, conspiracy, betrayal, and incompetence.

At a very basic level, we trust or distrust the inanimate objects around us. I'm not worried about my chair collapsing beneath me as I write this, but I know the kitchen door can trap my fingers if I'm not careful. That shelf isn't strong enough to hold the new TV, but those curtains will keep out the chill on a winter's night. Sometimes we're not sure whether to trust or distrust – will the car really survive a three-week tour of the Alps? – but usually time will tell.

At this level, trusting or distrusting things amounts to relying on them or not relying on them. This doesn't have the moral overtones or rich complexity of interpersonal trust and distrust. After all, I don't find myself grateful to the chair for its goodwill in holding me up, I don't accuse the kitchen door of betrayal when it pinches my fingers, and I'm not plunged into an existential crisis of trust if my car breaks down, though I may feel pretty frustrated. When you start to think your computer is conspiring against you, it's time to get some fresh air.

In this short book, I will focus on this richer form of interpersonal trust and distrust, stretched to include trust and distrust in social groups or institutions, like scientists, government, or the media. I will try to pinpoint what trust and distrust amount to, why and when we feel trust or distrust, and how we can become more effective, better trusters: when *should* we trust?

When considering trust, we also need to think about trustworthiness – the challenge of deciding who to trust is the challenge of working out who is trustworthy. And trustworthiness seems a noble aspiration for us all: it's a trait we respect in others, and try to encourage in our children. Trustworthiness looks like a moral virtue – part of being a good person – yet we know that there can be honour amongst thieves. The mafia don trusts his consiligeri implicitly, and they've earned this through their decades of trustworthiness. Trust and trustworthiness can oil the wheels of corruption and violence. Whilst you may not have first-hand experience of *omertà*, you will recognize the feeling of unwanted trust, of being made privy to unwelcome confidences. To understand the value of trust and trustworthiness, we will need to explore these darker byways, to see why something so valuable can sometimes be evil or at least unwelcome.

What is trust?

So what is trust? When we trust people, we rely on them. And there's an extra dimension to that reliance, something which differentiates true interpersonal trust from mere mechanical reliance on curtains, chairs, and cars. You can extend your mechanical reliance from mere objects to other people, relying on the crowd's mass to shelter you from the wind, or the unwitting busker to distract attention from your pickpocketing. But that kind of reliance isn't trust: if the crowd disperses, or the busker takes a break, they're not betraying you, or being untrustworthy. They're just not doing what you wanted or expected them to do:

they let you down, but only in the way that an unreliable car or a wobbly kitchen door can let you down.

You rely on the crowd and the busker, but without expecting them to take this into account – after all, they don't know you're relying on them. You don't expect to benefit from the goodwill of the crowd or the busker, or for them to care about your needs and feelings, you're just hoping to benefit from their presence. And that's why this doesn't amount to trust.

Let's change the example: suppose the busker is your accomplice, and you've agreed that he'll play for a good ten minutes, allowing you time to work your nefarious way around the whole crowd. You trust him, so you expect him to bear you in mind, to keep his promise because he knows you're counting on him; in return, he expects a share of the takings. And if he doesn't keep his side of the bargain, then he's betraying your trust, revealing that he's untrustworthy in this kind of situation.

So the difference between trusting someone and just mechanically relying upon them has something to do with your heightened expectations in trusting, and your reaction if the trustee lets you down. Researchers from different disciplines share this basic view of trust, but they can't agree about what exactly these heightened expectations and reactions are. Economists and social scientists tend to think in terms of rational self-interest: you trust people when you think it's in their own interests for them to help you, as when the busker expects a share of your immoral earnings. Philosophers tend to be more touchy-feely: you trust people when you think they are good-natured and caring towards you. Evolutionary psychologists tend to think that trust is about reciprocal altruism: you trust people so long as they don't let you down, since this is a stable, rewarding strategy for all concerned.

We'll see more of these different approaches to trust and trustworthiness in later chapters, but for the most part I will understand trust in terms of *commitment*: when we trust people, we rely upon them to meet their commitments. This commitment view of trust is quite flexible – after all, you might think that someone will meet their commitments to you because it's in their own interests to do so, or because they're good-natured and caring, or because reciprocal commitment-meeting is a good evolutionary strategy. And the view explains why we don't place 'interpersonal' trust in chairs, cars, and curtains: the curtains haven't made any commitment to keep out the cold air, after all. When we rely on a crowd as a windbreak, we realize that the crowd has made no commitment to shelter us, indeed they don't even know that's what we want. And that's why this isn't a matter of trust.

Differentiating trust

If you are lucky, there are one or two people you can trust absolutely. But not everyone is as lucky as you, and for the most part we trust different people, to different degrees, to do different things. I trust my colleagues to do their jobs competently, and to give me sensible advice about work matters, but I do not trust them for advice about my personal life. My children trust me to care for them when they're ill, but they do not trust me to choose the right Lego for them without strict supervision. We distinguish different realms of trust.

We also distinguish trust in people's skill from trust in their intentions: for full trust, both of these are required. For example, when I trust my colleagues to do their jobs competently, I trust that they have the relevant skills and ability, and I also trust that they are willing to put those skills into action. My trust would be undermined if I thought my colleagues were well-meaning incompetents – if I doubted their skill. And my trust would be undermined in a different way if I thought my colleagues were lazy or dishonest – if I doubted their intentions.

Trust involves expectations about skill and expectations about intentions to help – turning this around, trustworthiness requires both skill and good intentions. Being trustworthy is a matter of fulfilling our commitments – that's what's expected of us by the people who trust us. But this requires us to be judicious about accepting new commitments, as well as determined to fulfil the commitments we already have: the trustworthy person is brave enough to say 'no' to commitments she won't be able to fulfil.

Trust in deeds and trust in words

There are many things we can trust people to do, but speaking the truth is one of the most important. Think of all the things you know about the world around you, about the past, about distant lands, and about how other people feel and think. Now think about how much of that knowledge depends upon trusting what other people have told you – trusting your parents, your teachers, friends and acquaintances, the media, and so on. Even your knowledge of important facts about yourself – your date of birth, for example – depends upon your trusting other people to tell you the truth.

So any investigation of trust needs to encompass this special case of trust (or distrust) in what other people tell us. Trusting people requires us to trust in both their skill and their intentions, and the same holds of trusting what they say: this requires us to trust in people's knowledge, and trust in their honesty. We should not trust what people tell us if we think they don't have the relevant expertise; and we should not trust what people tell us if we think they are trying to pull the wool over our eyes.

Likewise, being trustworthy requires us to be sincere, but it also requires us to think before we speak, so that we do not present guesswork or speculation as firm fact: sincerity is not enough. Many people feel angry about Prime Minister Tony Blair's behaviour in the run-up to the 2003 invasion of Iraq, especially in the light of the 'dodgy dossier' which made the military threat from Iraq seem more serious than it eventually turned out to be. Blair protests his sincerity, his genuine belief that Saddam Hussein posed a significant threat. But even if we accept that Blair was sincere, this sincerity is not enough for trustworthiness – it's not enough to believe what you say, you also need to have good evidence to back it up, especially when the stakes are so high.

The twin requirements of sincerity and knowledge mean that the most trustworthy option is sometimes to say nothing, frustrating though that may be for listeners: with speech as with action, trustworthiness requires judiciousness in making commitments. If you don't know what you're talking about, don't say anything at all.

What is distrust?

Distrust isn't simply lack of trust. Sometimes we're just not sure whether to trust or distrust someone – we don't know the person well enough to judge her skill or her intentions. When we're undecided, we don't trust, but nor do we distrust.

At other times, neither trust or distrust is appropriate, and not because we're unsure which to choose. If I invite my best friend to a party, and she says she can't make it because she'll be on holiday, then I'll be disappointed of course. Do I trust her to show up at the party? No: I don't expect her to come. But this doesn't mean I distrust her in any way – after all, she's explained the situation honestly. This is a situation in which I neither trust nor distrust my friend to show up at my party: I simply expect her not to.

When we trust someone, we expect them to fulfil their commitments. When we distrust someone, we take them to have commitments but don't expect them to fulfil these commitments. My friend isn't committed to coming to my party – she says she can't make it. Because she has no commitment, there's no question about whether she will fulfil a commitment, so there's no question about whether to trust or distrust her in this respect.

Insisting on a distinction between distrust and absence of trust may seem like mere logic-chopping. Yet it's central to our moral judgements in this area. To distrust someone is to think less of them, to think of them as doing something wrong, however minor. Calling someone 'untrustworthy' is a moral criticism, and it's not something I'd like to hear about myself. But that doesn't mean I'd prefer to be drowning in others' trust, constantly expected to do as others prefer. Sometimes I want to be left alone with my own choices, without having others rely on me. I don't always want to be trusted, but I don't want to be untrustworthy either. In such circumstances, I crave the absence of trust, but I don't want the moral condemnation of being distrusted. And that's why it's important to distinguish distrust from mere absence of trust.

Deciding to trust?

A critical issue for all of us is who to trust, and why. What sort of evidence makes trust (or distrust) reasonable? And is evidence always necessary?

Thinking this way makes it seem as if trust is within our control, that we can consider the evidence, weigh it up, then decide who to trust about what. And maybe that's how it works sometimes. But often we simply find ourselves trusting one person and distrusting another, without having made a conscious choice in the matter. This can be very distressing: the realization that you distrust your partner or close friend may be a real shock, one that makes you re-evaluate your evidence in retrospect. Conversely, discovering that you trust a new friend or colleague can be a pleasant surprise, even if you can't say exactly why you feel this trust.

In these respects, trust and distrust are like belief and disbelief. Even if we try to base our beliefs on the evidence – as we should – this is not always a process of considering the evidence, deciding what to believe, and then believing it. Unlike other activities, believing doesn't seem to be within our direct control: I can decide whether or not to wait for the bus, but I cannot just decide whether or not to believe it will arrive soon.

French mathematician and philosopher Blaise Pascal acknowledged this when discussing the rationality of religious belief. Suppose that God exists. If you believe in Him, and live accordingly, you will benefit greatly in the afterlife. If you don't believe in Him, your post-death prospects are a lot bleaker: the torments of hell, in the worst-case scenario. Now, suppose that God does not exist. If you nevertheless believe in Him, that won't be any great loss to you, perhaps just some wasted Sunday mornings. And if you don't believe in a non-existent God, you don't stand to gain much. Taking all the possibilities into consideration, it looks as if our best bet is to believe in God: if He exists, this is definitely the best bet, and if He doesn't exist, it doesn't make much difference either way.

There's a lot to say about whether Pascal has calculated the odds properly in setting up his wager. But let's focus on what we should do if we accept his reasoning: suppose we agree that our best bet is to believe in God. Go on then, believe in God! If you already believe, you may be pleased to find the odds in your favour. But if you do not already believe in God – if you are agnostic or atheist – you cannot simply decide to start doing so when you find out that it's a good bet to do so. Belief doesn't seem to be something we can switch on or off at will, whenever it is convenient.

Pascal recognized this – indeed, his suggestion was that atheists and agnostics should begin to attend church, perform religious rituals, and hang out with true believers. That way, they were likely to become believers themselves. We can decide to put ourselves in a position where it's likely we'll start to believe something, but we cannot simply decide to start believing.

What about trust and distrust? Can we simply decide to trust? Sometimes we cannot decide to trust. If we firmly believe that someone is unreliable, we may decide to pretend to trust her, or decide to give her the opportunity to prove herself, but neither of these amount to genuine trust: when we put ourselves in the hands of someone we think is unreliable, we worry, we make back-up plans, and we're not surprised when she fails. These are signs of distrust rather than trust.

But there may be a middle ground where we can decide to move from uncertainty to trust. If we are genuinely unsure whether someone can be relied upon, we may decide to take our chances and trust her. Such trust can encourage trustworthiness when people react positively to being trusted, and this in turn can justify the original decision to trust. Parents must endure this, in taking difficult decisions about how far to trust their children at different ages: minimizing trust may minimize danger, but it also minimizes opportunities for children to develop and demonstrate their trustworthiness.

Researchers and thinkers from many academic disciplines have investigated trust, working in economics, management studies, anthropology, philosophy, biology, sociology, and more. And trust is something we've all encountered – and missed – in our everyday lives. Inevitably, there are many different conceptions of trust, and in different contexts, different aspects of trust will be important. But a number of key ideas run throughout: our trust in people and institutions is typically richer than our reliance on inanimate objects, and involves our expectation that commitments will be fulfilled. We can differentiate our trust, trusting someone to do one thing, but not to do another. Trust involves expectations about both competence and intentions; either alone is not enough for trustworthiness. In particular, trusting what people say involves trust in their knowledge as well as trust in their sincerity. Distrust is not just absence of trust: sometimes both trust and distrust are an imposition. We cannot simply decide to trust someone we believe is unreliable, but we can sometimes decide to shift from uncertainty to trust.

But trust – and distrust – are interesting primarily because they *matter*, and we should not go further with our explorations without looking at *why* they matter.

Chapter 2
Why trust and trustworthiness matter

The advantages of being trusted; the disadvantages of being distrusted

Life runs more smoothly when people trust you. A decent credit rating enables you to borrow money without paying punitive interest, a reputation for fair-dealing will help your small business flourish, and a plausible demeanour will help a great deal if you ever have to defend yourself in court.

Being distrusted excludes us from these advantages, and brings problems of its own. Convicted criminals struggle to find employment, wives of distrustful bullies can't sustain friendships or even conversations with other men, and young people from neighbourhoods and ethnicities distrusted by the police are liable to repeated, intrusive 'stop-and-search' procedures on the street.

Some of the benefits and harms generated by trust and distrust are practical – affecting our health, wealth, or enjoyment of life. But some strike more directly at who we are, at our personal integrity and autonomy. Distrust is an insult, not just an inconvenience; correspondingly, trust is a compliment. I want my friends, family, and colleagues to trust me, not just because that will make things go more smoothly for me – though it will – but also because I value their high opinion of me, and their level of trust is a key part of their opinion.

Now and again, we could wish for a little less trust. Trust carries expectations, even demands, and if we care about what others think of us, we may wish they would lower those expectations, so that we are not forced to choose between complying and disappointing. Trust can be a burden when we suspect we're not up to the job, that our best will not be good enough. And trust can be a burden when we simply don't want to do something: perhaps you'd rather your mother didn't trust you to call every evening when you get home from work, much as you appreciate her love and her confidence in you. Situations like this are tricky to handle: whilst you'd rather not be trusted in this respect, you don't want to be distrusted, or regarded as untrustworthy, either. Rather, you want your mother to stop thinking of your daily calls as a test of your trustworthiness.

On the whole, though, being on the receiving end of trust is a Good Thing, and being on the receiving end of distrust can be a very Bad Thing. All of us are both trusters and trustees, and as trusters we have some responsibility to get our trusting and distrusting right, so as to avoid damaging the innocent, and to avoid benefiting those who don't deserve our trust.

The advantages of trusting well; the disadvantages of trusting badly

When we trust, or distrust, we form expectations about what others will do and say, about their motives, capacities, and expertise. We paint a picture of our social world, and, for the most part, we're trying to paint an accurate picture, to work out who is genuinely trustworthy, and in which respects.

But we don't want an accurate picture simply for its own sake: we're not driven merely by intellectual curiosity about the trustworthiness of others. Getting it right about who to trust is a crucial practical skill, often hard-won. Distrusting the untrustworthy helps protect us from exploitation, disappointment, and betrayal. And trusting the trustworthy has positive advantages of its own, opening up the kinds of cooperative joint projects that are at the basis of marriage and friendship, flourishing businesses, rewarding professional lives, and successful sports teams.

Getting it right is also crucial to the mundane work of getting through the day safe and sound. We accept information from others, relying on unseen checks and standards: if we tried to assure ourselves of everything first hand, life would be impossible. The penalties for mistakes in trusting can be severe, but it's not an option simply to step back from the whole business of trust and distrust, at least not without stepping into a hermit's cave.

Just as we can benefit from receiving trust, we can benefit from offering trust, and these benefits extend past the merely practical aspects of making our lives run more easily. Surrounding ourselves with people we can trust just feels good, in a way that goes beyond pride in our own achievements at identifying these people. There is some pride in identifying a con-man for what he is, but finding a true friend is more rewarding.

From your own perspective, then, there is much to be gained from trusting the trustworthy, and distrusting the untrustworthy. But your own perspective is not the only one worth considering. Trust is a valuable commodity, and, as with any commodity, it can be distributed fairly or unfairly. If you trust only those people from the same ethnic background as you, or if you distrust all redheads, then you will lose out on many opportunities. But you won't be the only one who suffers; your behaviour is morally problematic because of the unfair damage it will cause to others.

What, then, do we owe to others in our trusting and distrusting? A simple answer is that we should trust the trustworthy, and

Why trust and trustworthiness matter

distrust the untrustworthy. It's hard to quibble with this as an ideal, but unfortunately, we cannot see into the souls of others to infallibly discern their trustworthiness or untrustworthiness in any given respect. Lacking such godlike powers, the best we can do is to make a fair assessment based on the evidence available to us, in the time available to us.

Again, it's hard to disagree with this as an ideal, but opinions may reasonably differ about what, if anything, the evidence shows and the time allows. Withholding judgement isn't always a realistic strategy, but rushing to judge can lead to serious error. And searching for more evidence, or asking for more time, can itself come across as a lack of trust, rather than a neutral attitude. In later chapters, we will explore some empirical studies about how we make these judgements, and reflect on how fair and accurate they are likely to be.

It's easy to see how lack of trust can damage its 'targets', but over-trust can sometimes be harmful too, whether or not it is welcomed by its receivers. Children often need to be protected from themselves – my kids think I should trust them to go to school unaccompanied, but in my view they're not old enough, and the route isn't safe enough. In these circumstances, I'm protecting them by not trusting them, though if I went too far – not trusting them even to play upstairs alone – I would harm, not help them, by hindering their development as responsible individuals.

It seems paternalistic to have similar concerns about adults, to worry about trusting them too much for their own good, but paternalism is sometimes the right attitude to take towards people who are struggling with overwhelming addiction, for example. There's no quick answer about where to draw the line in such cases: we need to balance the harm we do in over-trusting someone against the harm of undermining their autonomy and independence by under-trusting them.

So far, I have been writing as if 'trust the trustworthy, distrust the untrustworthy' were the ur-policy we should aim to follow, both for our own sakes and for those we target with our trust and distrust. We might on occasion have our doubts about how to implement this ur-policy, yet it remains our goal. But I have ignored a crucial complicating factor: communicating our trust can make people become more trustworthy, whilst communicating distrust can generate untrustworthiness. We're not dealing with a closed, unresponsive system: our judgements about trustworthiness are interventions which can have significant consequences.

In her 2002 Reith lectures, philosopher and public servant Onora O'Neill argued that a culture of suspicion has generated demands for accountability which have in turn undermined trust and professional responsibility, whilst consuming time and resources diverted from elsewhere. Economist Bruno Frey suggests that employers who monitor their employees' work rate too closely may have the perverse effect of reducing that work rate, as employees feel less trusted, and less inclined to demonstrate their skill and commitment. Given a baseline of at least moderate general goodwill, trust can become a self-fulfilling policy, and distrust likewise. This is unsurprising, given the idea that trust is a compliment, and distrust an insult: most of us respond to a little flattery.

There are limits. Some people will respond to proffered trust by exploiting the good intentions of the truster. Some people will respond to distrust with a determined resolve to prove their trustworthiness. Nevertheless, the consequences of interventionist trust must be weighed in the balance as we take our chances in social interaction.

Whether we can afford to err on the side of trustingness – and risk gullibility – depends on what's at stake, what we can afford to lose, and whose interests are involved. An employer may be admirable for offering a convicted criminal a second chance, but not if the employer is a school, and the convictions are for child abuse. More often than not, our decisions about trust will have consequences not only for the trustee, but also for those who depend upon us to make the right decision. Benefit of the doubt is not something we should easily offer on someone else's behalf. And those of us in positions of privilege may find it easier to take a chance with trusting, simply because the risks and stakes are lower for us.

Whether we can respond to trust by becoming more trustworthy – and risk being exploited – also depends upon what's at stake, and what our experience has taught us. People who are rarely trusted do not have the opportunity to develop their trustworthiness, and cannot be expected to respond with alacrity when trust is offered to them. This is one of the damaging elements of suffering from long-term distrust: in such an environment, it makes little sense to develop traits of trustworthiness, if these will go unrecognized. This in turn makes the habitually distrusted harder to trust, and the downward spiral continues.

High trust, low trust, and social capital

Trust benefits those who receive it, and distrust is a harm; conversely, there are many advantages to getting it right about (un)trustworthiness for those who offer trust. When others depend upon us, our decisions about trust can have far-reaching consequences, consequences we should take into account so far as we can. This is why trust and trustworthiness matter in interpersonal relationships, and for our everyday lives.

But many social scientists also believe that there are consequences for everyone of living in a 'high-trust' or a 'low-trust' society, consequences that affect each of us in ways which go beyond our individual relationships. 'Social capital' is set alongside physical capital (kit) and human capital (skills) in listing the resources that can make a society more or less productive. Social capital is a feature of social networks – the stronger the network, the greater the capital. It is reflected in levels of 'generalized reciprocity', our willingness to do favours for other people, in the expectation that, somehow or other, indirectly, we will eventually reap the rewards.

For example, I help a stranger who asks me for directions on the street. I do not expect to run into this particular stranger again when I'm visiting his home town, to call in the favour and get directions from him personally. However, I do have a generalized expectation that others will help me in similarly undemanding ways when I'm in my hour of need. Living in a society that is rich in such small favours and helpfulness is good for all of us – even for the freeriders who won't stop to help, but are happy to ask for help when they need it.

In general, if we can reasonably expect a decent level of honesty and cooperation from those we encounter in daily life, we can get on with our business without constant checking, locking, and worrying – whatever it is we're trying to get done, we can do it more productively and more easily. A shared student house is a society in microcosm. It's a nuisance to have the fridge clogged up with six separate milk cartons, even worse to have the bathroom cluttered with six separate toilet rolls. A better solution is to share the financial cost of such basic supplies, and to share the burden of remembering to shop. If the housemates can rely on one another each to pay and shop fairly regularly, so that these burdens are shared around informally, then they can get on with the more interesting aspects of student life. If instead a formal rota and kitty has to be established to ward off anarchy, it becomes a nuisance in its own right, especially if it has to be laboriously enforced.

Rotas and kitties are transaction costs that arise from a lack of trust amongst the housemates. Trust is an important aspect – though not the only aspect – of generalized reciprocity and social capital, and so trust has come to the attention of academics, policy-makers, and business people interested in the potential economic benefits of increasing trust. Organizational researchers – who often work in business schools – have explored the role and value of trust both within organizations and between them.

Trust, trustworthiness, and transaction costs are difficult to measure empirically, so we don't have hard-and-fast conclusions. But a comparative study of the Japanese and United States motor industries focused on relationships between large, powerful companies such as Ford and Toyota and the smaller specialized companies that supply them with components. Where suppliers reported high levels of trust, they were more willing to share information with buyers, and transaction costs were lower, both in terms of the length of pre-deal negotiations, and the monitoring of post-deal compliance. Confirming other studies, the researchers noted higher general levels of trust in Japan than in the United States.

Jeffrey H. Dyer and Wujin Chu, who ran the study, entitled their subsequent report 'The Role of Trustworthiness in Reducing Transaction Costs'. Why trustworthiness, not trust? Here, as in more intimate personal relationships, the importance of trust and trustworthiness stand and fall together. Trust is a benefit only where it is properly directed, towards those people or organizations that deserve our trust. Otherwise, trust becomes gullibility or naïveté, which is especially dangerous when others depend upon us, as do our employees, students, children, or customers.

Likewise, in thinking about our own lives, we should aspire to trustworthiness, as well as to wise trusting – trustworthiness is virtuous in its own right, but it is also crucial to the practical benefits of trust that we have explored in this chapter. Trust matters, but so does trustworthiness – these can form a self-reinforcing positive spiral, just as distrust and untrustworthiness can reinforce one another negatively. So how can we make sure we're in a positive, not a negative, spin? How can trust ever get started?

Chapter 3
Evolving trust and cooperation

Bats, bees, and chimpanzees

In the movies, vampire bats go out at night to feast upon the blood of innocent maidens, but in real life they stick to cattle and horses. Some nights, an individual bat is unlucky and returns to the communal roost hungry. Luckier bats charmingly vomit up some of the blood they've harvested, to feed their hungry colleagues. Why do they bother?

From an evolutionary point of view, these kindly vampires can seem very puzzling. Darwinian natural selection is characterized as the survival of the fittest: if some creatures manage to reproduce more than others, leaving more copies of their genes to the next generation, then those genes will spread throughout the population. So the creatures we see around us today – including the bats – result from many, many generations of sifting and sorting, a process favouring genes that increase reproductive success.

Becoming a blood donor doesn't directly increase an individual bat's chances of reproduction: instead, donation reduces its chances, by using up time and resources, and by enabling the recipient to live to compete another day with the donor for food and mates. It looks as if bats with a genetic disposition to donate blood would have less reproductive success overall than those without that genetic disposition, and so the practice would die out. But this doesn't happen. Why not?

Until the 1960s, biologists were keen on group selection. This is the idea that individual animals can make sacrifices for the good of their group, so that evolution would ensure the survival of the fittest group, even if individual members of the group lost out. Group selection seems to make sense of the kindly bats: overall, the colony of bats will flourish if hungry individuals are assisted by their fellows. But the group selection idea became less popular as biologists began to focus on selection at the level of the gene, rather than the group, or even the individual animal; this idea was developed by George C. Williams, and made famous by Richard Dawkins in *The Selfish Gene*.

The gene selection idea had many advantages, but one big disadvantage: it seemed unable to explain the apparently altruistic behaviour of vampire bats, and of certain social insects like worker bees. The workers spend their lives enabling the queen bee to reproduce, never having offspring of their own, and so it is hard to see why each generation doesn't simply contain more and more reproducing queens, with fewer and fewer sterile workers. How could the workers' genes persist in the population?

For the bees, the answer lies with family connections. The workers are the queen's daughters, and the larvae they care for are their brothers and sisters. We humans, and many other animals, typically share the same number of genes with our offspring as we do with our siblings. But a biological quirk means that worker bees are more closely related to their siblings than they would be to any offspring they might have: that is, they share more genes with their siblings than they would with any offspring. So it makes gene's-eye sense for the workers to look after those siblings: that's the best way to make sure their genes are passed down to the next generation.

22

This explanation – known as 'kin selection' – makes sense of creatures who appear to sacrifice their own interests in order to help their family. But that won't help explain the vampires, for they donate blood even when the recipient is only a very distant relative. The central puzzle is why genes for selfishness do not spread quickly through the bat population. Suppose there was one bat that did not donate blood to others. It could benefit from the donations of others, but refrain from helping them, and it looks as if this behaviour would pay off.

Scientists who dared study vampire bats night after night discovered that blood donation was not a one-way street: bats would donate one night, would be on the receiving end of bloody vomit on nights when they had been less successful, and would then in turn donate another night. Moreover, the bats seemed to keep track of who had helped them, who they had helped, and whether their help had been reciprocated. When help was not reciprocated, a bat would refuse to help that particular bat again in the future, though it was still willing to help others. This pattern of behaviour is known as 'reciprocal altruism': it is a kind of cautious helpfulness which punishes those who try to cheat the system.

The consequences of this kind of behaviour were explored in a simulation run by Robert Axelrod and William D. Hamilton. Fortunately, the researchers did not have to train up helpful and unhelpful bats, let them loose together, and see which ones managed to have more babies. Instead, they set up situations in which pairs of computers repeatedly had to 'decide' whether to help one another. Different computers were given different strategies: for example, some had the strategy of always being helpful, whilst others had the strategy of never helping. 'Tit-for-tat' strategists would always help on the first encounter with another computer, then in their subsequent encounters do whatever the other computer had done on the previous round.

If two tit-for-tat strategists encounter each other, each will begin by helping each other, then continue to cooperate in every subsequent round. The same goes if a tit-for-tat strategist meets a persistent helper, or if two persistent helpers meet. If a tit-for-tat strategist meets a persistent nonhelper, then in the first round there will be one-way help, and in subsequent rounds neither will help the other. If a persistent helper meets a persistent nonhelper, there will be a sequence of one-way, unreciprocated help.

In the simulation, each computer had an individual score of points which could go up or down: it costs points to help another, but the reward for being helped was larger than this cost. The average tit-for-tat strategist ended up with more points than the average persistent helper or the average persistent nonhelper. Why was this? Any encounter between tit-for-tat strategists and/or persistent helpers will profit both parties through mutual aid. But a persistent helper is liable to repeated exploitation by any persistent nonhelper it meets, whereas a tit-for-tat strategist will only fall for the persistent nonhelper once. So tit-for-tat strategists do better overall than persistent helpers. And tit-for-tat strategists also do better than persistent nonhelpers, who are safe from exploitation, but never get involved in profitable mutual aid.

If points were offspring, then tit-for-tat strategists would end up with more offspring than others, even in a mixed population where different individuals have different strategies. Those who try to 'cheat' – the persistent nonhelpers – will not prosper. This explains the behaviour of the vampire bats, who pursue what looks like a tit-for-tat strategy with their blood donation, giving blood when it is needed, but not if the hungry bat has previously failed to reciprocate. Tit-for-tat bats will have more offspring than persistently helpful or persistently unhelpful bats, and so this behaviour will spread through the population.

The conditions have to be right for tit-for-tat to succeed. First, there must be some limited resource that is worth more to the recipient than it is to the donor: the blood donation is a small sacrifice from the donor, but it could make the difference between life and death for the recipient. (This was reflected in the computer simulation: the cost of helping was lower than the reward gained from being helped.) Second, individuals must interact with each other repeatedly; and, third, they must be able to recognize each other: if the vampire bats couldn't tell each other apart, they wouldn't be able to track whether bats they'd donated to returned the favour later on. Fourth, individuals must be able to adjust their interaction with an individual depending on their past history together: if bats had an uncontrollable vomiting reflex when approached by hungry beggars, they wouldn't be able to punish those who didn't return their favours.

Chimpanzees seem to meet all these conditions. Frans de Waal and his collaborators have spent years observing captive groups of chimpanzees, first in Arnhem zoo in the Netherlands, then later at the Yerkes research centre in the United States. They recorded a highly developed system of reciprocal altruism within the group, with animals exchanging food and grooming services in a way which depends upon previous encounters. (Life in a human family with small children can sometimes feel like a one-way flow of food and grooming services.)

As the researchers note, however, captive chimpanzees have a generous supply of food and plenty of time for leisure and grooming; the food exchanges mostly concerned the extra treats introduced into the environment by the researchers. So we cannot straightforwardly infer from their behaviour under these circumstances to that in the wild, where 'altruism' may be more costly to the donor. Likewise, human beings living in straitened circumstances may struggle to make gestures that are easily afforded by those who are better off.

Social dilemmas

Like bats and chimpanzees, we human beings often face situations in which we must decide whether to help each other. Sometimes the decision is easy, because sometimes it's in my interest to do something which happens to help others, regardless of what they do. If I create a beautiful front garden for my own pleasure, then others will enjoy the view as they pass my house. The pleasure I get from my garden doesn't depend on what others do: their pleasure is incidental. If my neighbours also create beautiful gardens, then I will benefit from seeing them, but this doesn't affect what I get out of my own garden.

Well, that's lovely, and we should cultivate our gardens. But many social situations are more challenging than this. Suppose that a group of us fish from a small lake for a living. If we all fish moderately, stocks will be maintained, and we'll be able to go on making a living indefinitely. If we all fish greedily, there will soon be no fish left. It looks as if we should go for the moderate option. But wait: if everyone else fishes moderately, you can benefit from fishing greedily, without risk of exhausting the stocks. And if everyone else fishes greedily, the stocks will soon be exhausted whatever you do, so you might as well take the short-term benefits of being greedy. Whatever everyone else does, you are better off being greedy.

Situations like this are 'social dilemmas': when we consider everyone together, the best overall option is for everyone to cooperate, to fish moderately. If outsiders are concerned for the overall welfare of our community, they will want us all to fish moderately. But whatever the others do, each of us stands to gain personally by fishing greedily. The same fundamental social challenge is at the heart of many environmental problems. Why should I turn down the central heating to combat climate change? If nobody else turns down their thermostats, I might as well be comfortable while we await the apocalypse. And if the others do turn down their thermostats, they can save the planet whilst I sit cosily.

How could the outsiders try to encourage us all to fish moderately, or turn down our thermostats, to put the overall interests of the community ahead of our own personal interests? How could we as insiders try to achieve this? We do sometimes resolve social dilemmas – some natural resources are well managed, and we do sometimes make personal sacrifices for the general good. But how do we manage? What are the conditions and circumstances in which people manage to overcome narrow self-interest and cooperate with others?

Economist Elinor Ostrom was awarded the Nobel Prize in 2009 for her work on how property can be successfully managed locally without either central regulation or private ownership. At the prize-giving, she said, 'There's a five-letter word I would like to repeat and repeat and repeat: Trust.' For Ostrom, the conditions that can promote the development of such trust include a long-term situation, the opportunity to learn about others' reputations, and the possibility of communication between all the relevant parties.

Cheater detection

Perhaps the evolutionary arguments can help here, following the example of the bats and the chimpanzees. Have we evolved to use a tit-for-tat strategy in dealing with one another, because of the reproductive success such a strategy can bring? Human beings are the results of natural selection. This much is (or should be) uncontroversial. But it is highly controversial whether this fact can explain anything much about our individual or social behaviour, or our contemporary patterns of thinking. Many people are sceptical about such explanations, not least because evolutionary thinking about human beings has in the past often been used to serve disreputably regressive social ends. So we need to tread a cautious path of acknowledging our evolutionary heritage without automatically assuming that this heritage is the best or only explanation of every aspect of human behaviour and social interaction, and without assuming that if we have 'evolved to' do something then that morally justifies doing it.

Evolutionary psychologists think we can explain at least some aspects of our thinking and behaviour as the result of natural selection many thousands of years ago. The idea is that certain types of behaviour or patterns of thinking would have been advantageous in the period of our hunter-gatherer ancestors, that is, in the Pleistocene period which lasted from 2.6 million years ago to 10,000 BC. During that long period, genes favouring such advantageous behaviour or thinking would have become widespread in the population, and are likely to be with us still, influencing our thought and behaviour today. (Unfortunately for us, thinking and behaviour that worked well during the Pleistocene may not be quite so useful in the 21st century.) So if we can – somehow – establish what sort of thinking and behaviour would have been advantageous back in the day, that may help us identify and explain current patterns.

A classic example of this method is Cosmides and Tooby's discussion of the 'cheater-detection' module in the context of reciprocal altruism. Recall that a number of conditions need to be satisfied if tit-for-tat is to be a successful, stable strategy for dealing with other creatures. For the strategy to work, the creatures using it need to be able to recognize each other, to keep track of transactions, and to adjust their behaviour in the light of this history of transactions: they need to be able to penalize cheaters. Cosmides and Tooby argue that we do indeed seem to have a particular skill for keeping track of cheaters. The evidence comes from comparing our ability to keep track of abstract principles to our ability to keep track of social rules.

In tests, most people are not terribly good at thinking with 'if...then...' rules. Suppose you are confronted with four double-sided cards laid out on a table (as below).

Visible side of cards say:
• E
• G
• 3
• 8

Each card has a letter on one side and a number on the other, and your task is to check whether the following rule has been properly implemented: if a card has a vowel on one side, then it must have an odd number on the other side. Which card or cards do you need to turn over in order to check this rule? Take a moment to think about it.

Most people turn over either just the E card, or else the E card and the 3 card too. But the right answer is to pick up the E card and the 8 card. Why? E is a vowel, so you need to check that it has an odd number on the other side. 8 is *not* an odd number, so you need to check that it does *not* have a vowel on the other side: if there is a vowel, the rule has been broken. It doesn't matter what the 3 card has on the other side, because the rule doesn't say that *only* vowels can have an odd number on the other side.

Only one-quarter of people manage to get the right answer on that test. But if we change the details, the test seems to get a lot easier. Here are some more cards:

Visible side of cards say:
• beer
• juice
• aged 24
• aged 17

These cards describe four people in a bar; each card has a drink on one side, and an age on the other. Here's the rule: if a person is drinking beer, they must be 18 or over. Which card or cards do you need to turn over in order two check whether this rule is being followed? This time it's easier: you need to check the 'beer' card, to make sure it doesn't have an age below 18 on the other side. And you need to check the 'aged 17' card to make sure it doesn't have 'beer' on the other side. There's little temptation to check the 'aged 24' card, or the 'juice' card, since the rule doesn't say that people over 18 *have* to drink beer.

Three-quarters of people manage to get the right answer on this second test. Why the difference? In abstract terms, both tests have the same format: four cards, two sides each, and a rule of the form 'if dum dum dum, then dee dee dee'. Logically, there is no difference between the two tasks, yet we're better at the second than at the first. Further variations show that we're better at applying rules when they're about social norms, in particular when people must satisfy a condition (e.g. be over 18) in order to receive a benefit (freedom to drink beer).

In an intriguing twist, researchers tested both bosses and workers about the following rule: if someone works on the weekend, then that person gets a day off during the week. Workers were excellent at spotting cheating bosses: had anyone worked on the weekend but not had the day off they were entitled to during the week? Bosses, on the other hand, paid very little attention to this. Instead, they checked whether anyone had taken a day off during the week without working on the weekend, even though this is not explicitly forbidden by the stated rule (a worker might be entitled to a day off during the week for good performance, for example). We're all good at spotting cheaters, but what counts as cheating depends on where you're standing.

Tit-for-tat writ large

So we have a knack for detecting cheaters. If we know the facts, and we know the rule, we all have the petty official's talent for putting these together to spot wrongdoing. And this is one of the prerequisites for 'tit-for-tat' to be a successful strategy in a population where we face repeated social dilemmas – if we are to sacrifice our short-term self-interest for the longer-term collective success, we will need to detect and punish cheaters to ensure the contribution of other people to this collective success.

But there are several other requirements for tit-for-tat: limited resources, repeated interaction, ability to recognize other individuals, ability to adjust our behaviour in response to that of others. (These look like the very conditions Elinor Ostrom connects with trust in local communities.) In the modern world, many of our collective projects involve us with people we will never meet – for example, trying to combat climate change, to protect fish stocks, or to maintain a safe environment on the street. The apparatus of the state, via the police, the legal system, and government, is crucial to creating the right conditions for tit-for-tat, since we as individuals are rarely able to identify and punish those who do not cooperate in these large enterprises. (And this isn't just a practical issue: there are very good reasons to avoid summary citizen justice outwith the legal system.) Indeed, many of these issues reach beyond national boundaries, creating difficulties on a grand scale. Our cheater-detection module can only take us so far.

Finally, what does reciprocal altruism, enabled by cheater detection, have to do with trust, distrust, and trustworthiness? Tit-for-tat players, whether bat, chimp, or human, begin by doing a favour for someone, in the hope that this will be reciprocated; if it is not, then no more favours are forthcoming. We could describe this as an act of trust, trust which is terminated if it is betrayed because the recipient of the favour turns out to be untrustworthy.

Alternatively, we could describe this in terms of calculated risk: the favour-giver makes a small gamble on predicting her fellow creature's future behaviour. If she gets it right, it increases her confidence in future gambles of the same kind. If she makes a mistake, she is wise enough not to throw good resources after bad.

Calculated risk-taking and trusting are not quite the same, though trusting can often involve risk-taking. Turn the picture around, and think about what obligations the recipient has. If someone does you a favour out of the blue, without you asking for this, you ought to be grateful. But trustworthiness doesn't oblige you to reciprocate, so long as you're open about this – there's nothing dishonest about saying 'thanks very much, but I can't return the favour'. To be sure, this can feel awkward, which is one reason we sometimes prefer not to receive favours. But being a trustworthy person doesn't require you to cooperate with everyone who wants to cooperate with you, to make sure that everyone who takes a chance on you reaps the reward. Trustworthiness requires you to meet your commitments; it doesn't always require you to meet other people's expectations or hopes.

Moreover, if someone does you a 'favour' purely in the calculated expectation that you will scratch their back in return, this won't feel like you are being trusted. Even if you're happy to return the favour, this won't necessarily feel like a trusting relationship, as opposed to a mutually convenient arrangement. Trust, and trustworthiness, may develop from such beginnings, but successful interaction doesn't always exemplify trust.

It can be a useful short-hand to think about these interactions in terms of trust and trustworthiness, but if we do so, we should bear in mind the very wide variety of meanings which 'trust' can bear. There is no simple step from vomiting bats to the trust and distrust we find in complex interpersonal relationships, where moral categories, and feelings of resentment, pride, and anger, are easily invoked, and we are able to take on explicit commitments to one another.

Chapter 4
Take the money and run

Playing the trust game

You're at an unfamiliar bar, chatting to a new acquaintance, Daniel, when an economist approaches with a glint in her eye and a wallet full of cash. She offers you ten dollars – the money is yours to keep, and you can pocket it right away if you like. But you have another option. If you give some or all of the ten dollars to Daniel, the economist will triple the gift – if you hand over four dollars, the economist will add another eight, so that Daniel gets a total of twelve dollars. Daniel can then keep the lot, or else decide to give some or all of it back to you.

Your first reaction is to suspect a trick – after all, who gives out free money in bars? Is Daniel in on this somehow? But the economist shows you her credentials – her experimenter's licence from the university, her membership card for the American Economics Association – and the barman confirms that she comes in every night, offering cash and choices, and following through on her promises. So you take the ten dollars she's offering.

What next? Will you give some to Daniel, hoping he'll return it with interest once the economist has tripled the sum? It's a risk: you need to predict what Daniel will do, but you barely know him.

It looks as if the rational thing will be for Daniel to keep whatever he gets, so maximizing his gain. After all, by that stage, he'll have the cash in hand, and giving some back to you will only make him worse off. And if he's going to keep whatever he gets, you should keep your ten dollars and end the game there.

But that would be a shame – that way, you get ten dollars and Daniel gets nothing. If you hand him four, which the economist turns into twelve, then he might split it, returning six (making a total of twelve for you) and keeping six for himself; collectively, you will have taken eighteen dollars from the economist, not just ten. You can both benefit if you take a chance on Daniel and he responds as you hope. So what will you do?

Economists don't, as a rule, hang out in bars trying to give money to strangers. But they do persuade universities to let them hang out in labs trying to give money to students. The scenario I've just described is called the 'basic trust game', and it is arranged so that the participants are hidden from one another and can't communicate. Moreover, they are told that they will be playing as a one-off, with no chance to build up a rapport over several rounds. What choices do you think people make?

When thirty-two participants were given the initial ten dollars, an amazing thirty decided to hand over at least some money, and the average amount they gave was a bit more than five dollars. That left thirty lucky recipients deciding whether to simply pocket the cash and leave, or else send some back to their 'investor'. Twelve made for the exits, but eighteen decided to send back at least a dollar, and, of those, eleven sent back more than they'd originally been given (before the economist tripled it), ensuring that the investor would make a profit. On average, investors who sent more than five dollars were rewarded for their generosity by getting back more than they sent, whilst investors who sent less than five dollars typically made a loss on the deal.

These games enable student guinea-pigs to squeeze a few dollars out of their professors. But that's not their main purpose. To the researchers, the results suggest that:

- trust is risky;
- trust can benefit the truster;
- when one person trusts another, both can profit;
- people don't always follow what looks like their own self-interest;
- people don't expect others to follow what looks like their own self-interest.

How does all this follow from students swapping dollar bills with strangers in a lab?

- *trust is risky*: of the thirty people who decided to hand over some of their initial cash, twelve lost out when the recipients simply pocketed the whole tripled lot;
- *trust can benefit the truster*: some of the people who initially handed over money got back more than they had invested, so took home more than the original ten dollars;
- *when one person trusts another, both can profit*: when money changed hands, extra money entered the game, because the economist tripled the transfer, and in some cases this extra money was shared between the participants;
- *people don't always follow what looks like their own self-interest*: eighteen of the thirty cash recipients volunteered to give some of it back, with no obvious benefit to themselves;
- *people don't expect others to follow what looks like their own self-interest*: thirty of the original thirty-two took the risk of hoping their recipient would voluntarily return some cash, even though it was not clear how this would benefit the recipient.

From an everyday perspective, these results aren't so very surprising. Most of us are all too familiar with the riskiness of trust, having endured faithless lovers, dodgy traders, or conniving colleagues (the unluckiest of us have suffered all three). Yet we know that when people work together trustingly, they can get a lot more done, to the benefit of all concerned. And few of us are cynical enough to expect others to be motivated by pure self-interest alone. Does the basic trust game tell us anything new?

What the game results show is that this sort of behaviour is widespread even in the entirely artificial situation of the lab, where people are playing with strangers for small amounts of cash, following unfamiliar rules, with a guarantee of no follow-up or reputational damage. Even in these weird circumstances, it's completely normal for people to take the chance of trusting a complete stranger to return money to them voluntarily; and it's quite common for that trusting gamble to pay off.

The games allow researchers to put numbers on trusting and trustworthy behaviour – to calculate rates of return on trusting investments, to record numbers of cooperators and noncooperators, and so on. And numbers are useful because they allow us to compare the consequences of setting the game up in different ways, or under different circumstances, perhaps with different nationalities or different age groups. This may help us work out the influences on trusting behaviour: what makes us more likely to trust, or more likely to be trustworthy, and what circumstances encourage distrust.

Variations on the basic trust game

In the basic trust game, those on the receiving end have a strong incentive to take their tripled cash and run, instead of giving some back to a stranger they'll never see again. But what if they knew this was to be the first of several rounds of the game?

In a follow-up study – with different students – all participants were told they'd be playing two rounds of the game: the economist provides ten dollars, triples anything that is transferred to the second player, and waits to see if any is returned. She then provides another ten dollars to the original player, and the game is run again.

This time, absolutely all the original players handed over some money, and almost half of them sent the whole lot. (Why were they more generous than in the one-round trust game? They could work out that the recipient had a financial incentive to cooperate, to increase their chances of being trusted in the second round.) And their generosity paid off: almost all the recipients returned more than the original player had sent them (the tripling meant they still made a profit on this first round).

Second round. Those few original players who'd lost out in the first round decided not to throw good money after bad, so ended the game there. Once bitten, twice shy. Almost all the rest sent some money, willing to take the chance that their partners would reciprocate for a second time. But more than half were disappointed, receiving less than they'd sent: plenty of recipients returned money in the first round but not the second.

So people's behaviour in the first round is highly cooperative – the recipients sensibly try to establish a good reputation, and this is what the original players expect them to do. When they get into the second, final round, much of this falls away, and people are more inclined to look to their own short-term interest. Even so, quite a few recipients returned money in the second round.

Other variations on the basic trust game involve giving the participants more information about each other. It turns out that a smile really does help the world go round: original players were significantly more likely to hand over some money to a recipient when they'd seen her smiling in a photo. And knowing that you're playing with someone from your team makes you more likely to hand over the cash: students at the University of California, Los Angeles were much more cooperative when they thought they'd been paired up with a member of their own fraternity.

The easily quantifiable nature of these games also enables researchers to do international comparative studies. Social psychologist Toshio Yamagishi has explored a number of comparisons between US and Japanese responses to variants on the trust game. He argues that Japanese people tend to rely more upon social structures and sanctions to back up agreements, making them less likely to trust strangers in artificial lab situations where no such sanctions apply. This contrasts with the idea, promoted by other researchers, that Japanese culture encourages people to be generally more trusting than does US culture; for Yamagishi, any differences are due to different safeguards in Japanese society, not different basic dispositions to trust.

Finally, 'neuroeconomist' (he invented the term) Paul Zak has examined the hormones of people playing the trust game, and the results are intriguing. Original players who get a dose of oxytocin via nasal spray are more likely to hand over a significant amount of cash, whilst receiving cash in the game boosts oxytocin levels, although receiving cash simply as a result of chance does not have this effect. Oxytocin is sometimes known as the 'cuddle chemical', as it is associated in both humans and other animals with bonding and social contact. But oxytocin also has a more sinister aspect: psychologist Carsten De Dreu found that white Dutch subjects who got a whiff of the hormone were more likely to associate positive words with pictures of other white people, and negative words with pictures of Middle Eastern people. Meanwhile, psychologist Carolyn Declerck showed that oxytocin boosted cooperation amongst people who already knew each other, but decreased cooperation amongst strangers.

What's trust got to do with it?

But do these games really tell us anything about trust and distrust? Go back to the bar: the economist has given you ten dollars, and you're trying to decide whether to give some of this to Daniel, in the hope that he'll return to you some of the tripled sum. What's Daniel doing while you're thinking? He wants you to hand over some cash, so he's put on a winning smile, he's trying to strike a deal, he's promising on his mother's grave to return some of the cash. And you need to decide whether to trust his protestations. If you do trust him, but he reneges on the deal and keeps the lot, you're entitled to feel cheated, even resentful: he broke a promise!

In the lab, none of this is possible. The participants don't get to negotiate, the original player doesn't get to ask the other what he'll do, and in return he doesn't get to offer any promises or swear on his mother's grave. If the original player takes a chance, hands over some cash, and doesn't get any return, then she will certainly feel disappointed. But has she been cheated? Let's interview the recipient: will he admit that he's done something wrong, betrayed trust, acted dishonestly? No: he'll surely argue that if people want to give him money out of the blue, that's their look-out. He never said he'd hand any back, and so why should he?

In Chapter 1, I distinguished between the rich, interpersonal trust we sometimes place in one another, and a more mechanical reliance we can invest in inanimate objects: I rely on my car to get me to work, but I don't feel cheated or betrayed by the car if it breaks down one morning (though I may feel cheated by the guy who sold it to me). In contrast, rich trust involves expecting commitments to be fulfilled.

In the bar, you have to decide whether Daniel is likely to meet the commitments he's making. But in the lab, the participants simply don't make any commitments to one another. The original participant takes a chance, trying to guess how the recipient will respond, but this is more like gambling on a horse than engaging in an interpersonal relationship.

This may explain what happened when Oregon school pupils played the trust game. The youngest children – eight-year-olds – were the stingiest about passing on the money experimenters gave them, and even the older children were typically stingier than adults. This surprised researchers: don't we usually think of children as more trusting than adults, and younger children in particular? But if we think of original participants not as trusting but as gambling or investing in the hope of future returns, then this makes perfect sense: it's a rare child who can hold out for delayed gratification.

Moreover, it's not clear that original players are guided by financial motives alone. As the 'dictator game' shows, people will sometimes hand over money even when there is no possibility of a return. In this game, the original participant is given ten dollars, and invited to choose between keeping the lot, or giving some to the other participant. Either way, that's the end of the game, and there's no second round.

Somewhat surprisingly, one-third of the participants handed over some cash, even when they were guaranteed absolute anonymity: not even the experimenters would be able to match individuals with decisions. When participants felt they could be identified, they were more generous: four out of five handed over at least some money. These results suggest that there's more going on in the trust game than just calculation of the odds, that people's decisions about handing over money don't just depend upon what they expect to get in return. (Children are particularly mean in the dictator game.)

And think about the artificiality of these situations. For a start, the amounts of money are relatively small. No-one risks going to bed hungry, or even leaving the lab with less money than they arrived with. As the philosopher Russell Hardin points out, an initial stake of $10,000 rather than ten dollars might induce quite different results. (It's hard to imagine universities funding such expensive research, but it might make for a good TV game show.) Because of the low stakes, fun and curiosity may play a role in decision-making: there may be some tendency for original participants to 'play along', rather than just pocketing the cash and ending the game. (Those Oregon children might have taken ten dollars a lot more seriously than adults do, but in fact they were allowed a stake of just one dollar, in tokens which could be exchanged for toys at the experimenters' store, a system known in other circumstances as 'truck'.)

Finally, participants must decide whether to believe what the experimenters tell them about the set-up. Are they really playing other human beings, as opposed to computer programs? Are they really playing anonymously? Will there really be only one round of the game? Will the transfer really be tripled? Will they really be allowed to take this cash home? If there is any genuinely rich interpersonal trust in these games, it is invested in the experimenters.

Uneasiness about the artificiality of the lab experiments, and uncertainty about quite what they're testing, has led a number of researchers to set the game results alongside a quite different approach to the empirical study of trust: public opinion surveys.

Surveys

For nearly 40 years, pollsters have been asking Americans: 'Generally speaking, would you say that most people can be trusted, or that you can't be too careful in dealing with people?' Well, what do you reckon?

More and more Americans are inclined to think that you can't be too careful in dealing with people. But this is not because individual citizens are changing their minds: on the whole, earlier generations have maintained their trusting attitudes as they've aged, but younger generations, who are less trusting, are also maintaining their distrust as they age. Trusters are dying off, and distrusters are taking over.

This is a striking trend. But what does it mean? Like any such survey, it relies on people to have a good level of self-knowledge, and to report that knowledge honestly. Most of us don't spend much time thinking about whether, in general, other people can be trusted, and so it may be quite hard to know exactly what we believe if asked on the street by a stranger (who is inviting our trust). Moreover, most of us don't want to seem either gullible or paranoid, so our responses may depend partly on what we think other people – of our own generation? – would say. And the way in which we respond to what we think others will say will vary too: you may like to think of yourself as an open person, more trusting than the average, whereas I value the idea that I am a hard-nosed sceptic.

Beyond these general concerns, there's a particular problem with the survey questions about trust: they're incredibly vague and ambiguous. Most people? Which most people? Most people you know personally, most people you pass in the street, most politicians, most doctors, most people in the country? And dealing with people? What sort of dealing? Financial transactions, accidentally jostling someone on the bus, going on a blind date, getting married, letting your teenager throw a party while you're away? Whether or not you're inclined to trust surely depends on what's at stake, and who you're dealing with.

Despite the limitations of such questions, researchers have sometimes put them to participants in the 'trust games', where people take chances on offering money to their partners, in the hope of getting more in return. We might expect that willingness to take a chance on others in those games would go along with the view that most people can be trusted. After all, why would you hand over money to a stranger, if you believed that you can't be too careful in dealing with people?

Weirdly, it turns out that people who agree that most people can be trusted are no more likely to hand over money in the trust game; some experiments even suggest that they are *less* likely to hand over money than those who think you can't be too careful. On the other hand, people who agree that most people can be trusted turn out to be more trustworthy recipients of cash: if you think that others can be trusted, you are more likely to respond to others' trust in you, and return some of your tripled gains to the original participant.

So if someone says he's a trusting kind of guy, it's a good bet that he won't take a chance on other people returning his cash, but he will cooperate with you if you trust him. This is most peculiar: the 'trust' games and the 'trust' survey questions both have their strengths and weaknesses, but whatever they're measuring, it's not the same thing.

Trust, risk, and cooperation

The game experiments don't tell us much about the kind of rich trust we have with our friends and family (if we're lucky), because of the artificiality of the situations, and their low stakes. Nor do they tell us much about the kind of trust we might have in politicians, doctors, or social institutions, where the stakes are high, and we do have access to certain kinds of information both about track records and about the characteristics of these people and institutions. As I argued earlier, someone who doesn't return any money in these games may well be disappointing the original participant, but it's hard to see this as dishonesty or betrayal.

Perhaps a better way of thinking about trust games is in terms of cooperation, or doing things for others. The dictator game – where the original participant either keeps the cash or hands some over with no hope of return – shows that at least some of us will do something for a stranger, especially if we think our generosity or stinginess will be made public. In the basic trust game, the original participant gets to help the recipient, and hopes that the recipient will help her in return: when this works out well, both are better off than they would have been without any handover.

The ultimatum game highlights the dark side of all this lovely help and cooperation. This game is like the dictator game, except that if the recipient decides she hasn't been given enough cash, she can opt to have all the money confiscated by the experimenter. From one perspective, it looks as if the recipient should simply accept whatever she's given, since any amount is better than none. But in fact, student subjects are willing to sacrifice their own share to punish stinginess. Indeed, participants expect this: in lab tests, the most typical move is to offer the recipient a 'fair share', a full half of the original ten dollars. It's hard to see any of this in terms of trust.

Joseph Henrich and his collaborators have invited people to play the ultimatum game in a range of small-scale non-industrialized societies across the world, from Paraguay to Papua New Guinea: they find a wide variety of responses, which they correlate with differences in social and economic structures in the different societies. Unlike their counterparts on campuses in the developed world, Henrich's researchers were able to offer participants in the game an original stake of a day or two's wages, either in cash or as tobacco or other goods; this already changes the nature of the game. In some groups, such as the Tsimané of Bolivia, original participants typically offered quite a meagre share of their allocation, but this was invariably accepted by the recipient. In other groups, such as the Gnau of Papua New Guinea, many recipients rejected both 'hyper-fair' (more than 50%) and unfair offers. The researchers note that the Tsimané live in small family groups, and rarely need to cooperate with anyone outside the family. The Gnau recognize gifts as committing the recipient to reciprocate at a time chosen by the gift-giver, meaning there is a potentially large cost to accepting gifts.

It looks as if people's behaviour in these artificial games is influenced, naturally enough, by the costs, benefits, and mechanisms available for cooperation and reciprocation in the societies in which they live; the same goes for the college students

44

who are the more typical subjects of research. Cooperation is important, even when it doesn't involve trust, strictly speaking. And 'trust' games allow us to attach numbers to people's behaviour in these different situations, which in turn allows us to quantify how people's behaviour changes as the circumstances change. This may tell us something about which conditions encourage cooperation, and which do not. And this in turn can help us learn about the conditions for the more complex forms of trust we also value.

Trustworthiness, thought of as a moral virtue we admire in others, and try to teach to our children, is a matter of living up to our commitments and promises, not just a matter of doing what other people would like us to do. You can be trustworthy without being terribly generous, so long as you follow through when you do offer to help. And you can be kind and generous without being terribly trustworthy, if you have a habit of over-committing yourself, and having to let people down. But the whole structure of commitment, obligation, virtue and vice presupposes a basic level of cooperation, of the type which can be illuminated even by the artificial dollar-swapping games to which generations of students – and a fair number of nomads, foragers, and whale-hunters – have been subjected.

Chapter 5
Honesty and dishonesty

Trusting what someone says has two aspects: an expectation of honesty, and an expectation of knowledge. If I trust my son when he says that his school is closed today, then I trust that he is honestly expressing his belief, and I also trust that he knows what he's talking about. Either alone isn't enough. If I think he's lying, then I won't trust what he says. And if I think he's persuaded himself through wishful thinking instead of seeking evidence, then I won't trust what he says either (though I will forgive wishful thinking more easily than a lie).

Likewise, trusting someone to do something has two aspects: an expectation of good intentions, and an expectation of skill or ability. If I trust my daughter to choose a healthy lunch at school, then I trust that she will do her honest best to make a healthy choice, and also that she's capable of telling healthy from unhealthy choices. Either alone isn't enough. If I think she doesn't care about healthy food, I won't trust her to make the right choice. And if I think she can't tell the difference between healthy and unhealthy food, then again I won't trust her to make the right choice. She might choose a healthy lunch by chance, but I can't trust her to do so.

Distrust comes in correspondingly different forms. When I'm sceptical about the medical advice a friend offers me, I don't doubt her honesty and good intentions but I do doubt her expertise.

When I'm sceptical about the medical advice the pharmaceutical company offers me, I don't doubt their expertise, but I do doubt their good intentions.

Our judgements about honesty, or good intentions, are more morally weighty than our judgements about knowledge or skill. Sometimes we hold people morally or even legally responsible for their ignorance – they should have known better! – but, as I do with my son, my daughter, and my friend, it is much easier for us to forgive an honest, even careless, mistake than a deliberate deception.

Dishonesty invites condemnation and resentment, but lack of good intentions is a more subtle matter. Part of growing up is the realization that the world doesn't owe me a living: many decent people are simply indifferent to me, and won't go out of their way to make my life easier. And, unless I am in dire need, there are limits on what other people are obliged to do for me: it would be nice if a passer-by tidied up the litter which has blown into my front garden, but passers-by aren't obliged to do these sort of favours, no moral crime is committed when they walk on by, and I should not resent them for doing so (though I'm entitled to resent those who dropped the litter in the first place).

This is why it's useful to think of trust and distrust in terms of commitment. I can predict, or guess, whether the next passer-by will pick up the litter – perhaps I know that my approaching neighbour can't stand to see an untidy garden. I can appreciate and thank the passer-by who picks up the litter, and I can be disappointed by the passer-by who doesn't. But it would be unfair to regard one as more trustworthy than the other on these grounds – more helpful, more generous, more community-spirited, perhaps, but not more trustworthy. Why? Because neither has promised or committed to pick up litter from my garden, and neither is under an obligation to do so. You yourself may wish you had time to do more for your neighbourhood, and you may feel bad about that, but you needn't feel *untrustworthy* unless you've actually offered to go out and help, and then failed to do so.

So trust involves an expectation of honesty – an expectation that someone will do their best to meet their commitment to you – and an expectation of knowledge, skill, or ability. We judge and value these two aspects in quite different ways; this chapter will focus on honesty (and dishonesty), while the next will focus on knowledge (and ignorance).

Lie detection

How good are we at spotting liars? Psychologists have run studies in which people are asked to judge whether strangers are lying or telling the truth. Overall, people tend to make the right judgement about 54% of the time. Not bad? Not good: given the set-up, a simple coin-toss – heads he's lying, tails he's telling the truth – would give a 50% success rate, so 54% isn't a great achievement. There is a tendency to over-estimate honesty in these cases: it's more common to believe a liar is honest than to wrongly accuse someone of lying.

Perhaps unsurprisingly, it is harder for people to make the right judgement when they can see but not hear the speakers; beyond that, it doesn't make much difference whether people are looking and listening, just listening, or even just reading a transcript of what's said. Overall, people were more likely to believe speakers they could hear, regardless of whether they could also see the speaker. Observers detected children's lies more easily than they detected adults' lies, but this seems to be due to a predisposition to think that children are more likely to be lying than adults.

In many of these studies, the speakers are assigned randomly to lie or speak truthfully about some artificial situation which doesn't matter much to either speaker or listener. But in real life, we make judgements about motivation when we're trying to judge honesty. What's in it for her? Why might she be trying to trick me? What has she got to gain or to lose? This is why we're suspicious of people who are trying to sell us something. Some researchers tried to make the situation more realistic, by rewarding speakers who managed to persuade listeners they were telling the truth. Ironically, this made them look less honest, whether or not they were lying: the more you want to be believed, the more suspicious you look!

When these sorts of studies began to be published in the 1980s, the phones started to ring. Psychologist Paul Ekman was invited to speak about his work on lie detection to groups including polygraphers from the CIA, FBI, NSA and military, the US Secret Service, judges, police members of the California Robbery Investigators Association, and psychiatrists. He took advantage of this access to try out the truth-or-lie tests on these specialist groups, and discovered that only the Secret Service agents did significantly better than the rest of us. Ekman and his co-author Maureen O'Sullivan speculate that work in close protection, which involved scanning crowds for threats, may have helped the agents develop their skills.

Ekman later inspired Tim Roth's character in the TV series *Lie to Me* – Dr Cal Lightman has super-scientific lie-detection skills, picking up on the tiniest change in facial expression, tone of voice, or body language. He helps fight crime, whilst trying to resist the temptation to become a mega-liar himself. But, as the Fox website relates, 'his scientific ability is both a blessing and a curse in his personal life ...'. Who'd have thought it?

Ekman himself was a consultant on the TV series, and has said that most of the techniques it portrays are accurate, though the fiction makes it all look quicker and easier than it is in real life. He rejects as unethical Lightman's use of lies to provoke others into revealing themselves, whilst noting other differences between Lightman and himself: 'He's younger, edgier, arrogant, brusque, and he's English'.

Just like the lab-based experiments on 'trust' which involved exchanging relatively small cash sums in artificial situations, experiments on lie detection have significant limitations, as the researchers themselves realize. First, they are often conducted between strangers – the experimental subjects are typically shown video footage of someone they've never met before. It may be that we get better at 'reading' people the longer we know them, and have independent evidence about whether they have previously lied. Second, in real life, we often use our background knowledge to assess the truth or falsity of what's said – is the claim a good fit with what we already believe? If not, is this person likely to be an overriding authority on the subject matter? In the artificial experimental situations, audiences do not have access to relevant background information either about the subject matter or about the speaker's credentials. In some cases, the audience doesn't even get to know what's being said: they are asked to judge the speaker by visual cues alone. Third, it's known on all sides that these are artificial situations, so it may be that the standard moral or socially imposed requirement to tell the truth is suspended for a while. Finally, audiences in the experiments are asked to make explicit judgements about whether the speaker is lying or telling the truth: in everyday situations, at least when the stakes are low, we may simply assume that others are telling the truth without even considering the possibility of a lie. If asked to reflect, we might become more cautious.

So we shouldn't think that these experiments give us the whole truth about lying, interesting though they are. But it's difficult to make a proper scientific study of lying and lie detection in the field: there are so many factors at work, and the neutral observer often just can't tell whether people are lying, or whether they are believed.

Psychologists Nancy Darling and Bonnie Dowdy studied pairs of mothers and their adolescent offspring, trying to assess the degree to which they trusted one another in areas where they disagreed, such as choice of friends, use of leisure time, drinking alcohol, or smoking. An initial hurdle became apparent when they realized that many mother–adolescent pairs disagreed about what they disagreed about. But once that was accounted for, Darling and Dowdy found that mothers were typically over-suspicious, assuming deception when in fact the adolescent was telling the truth, but quick to spot real lies. For their part, the teenagers who felt most trusted by their parents were the teenagers who accepted that their parents had the right to set rules and boundaries for them.

Cues and confidence

One advantage of the lab-based studies is that participants can be invited to reflect on their judgements, and how they make them, and these reflections can be compared with the participants' actual accuracy. In some cases, participants were asked how confident they were in their judgements, how likely it was that they had spotted the liars, and not falsely accused any of the truth-tellers. Although in fact most people do only slightly better than chance, most of us tend to think we are pretty shrewd. This suggests that we're much too confident in our own skills. The studies even reveal that the worse people are at telling truth from lies, the more confident they are that they're getting it right – self-confidence is highest amongst those who are worst at judging truth from lies. (Men are significantly more confident in their judgements than women are, though they are no more accurate.) So a first step towards becoming a better lie-detector is learning to question your own judgement on the matter.

Why is this? One reason is that people are in general overconfident in their skills, especially with respect to fairly difficult tasks, and lie detection is a difficult task. Most of us think we're above-average drivers, that we are better at our jobs than our workmates, and that we're doing a better job raising our kids than our neighbours are doing with theirs. Obviously, I'm right about my own case, but we can't all be above average (except in Lake Wobegon). A second reason is that most of us have ideas about what a liar looks like – shifty gaze, sweaty brow, fidgety manner – but most of us are simply wrong about this. We're relying on a false theory, but we think it's just great, and that increases our confidence in our own judgement about who's telling lies.

Can we do better? There are no universal tells, behavioural tics that inevitably accompany lying, and yet never appear in innocent circumstances – as the experts say, there's no 'Pinocchio's nose'. But there do seem to be some fallible clues in our behaviour. Paul Ekman (aka Dr Cal Lightman) and Wallace V. Friesen distinguish leakage cues and deception cues. Leakage cues provide brief glimpses of what the speaker is really thinking or feeling. Deception cues – signs of tension – are signs that the speaker is trying to mislead, but they don't indicate what's underneath the cover-up. Overall, we might expect lying to be more stressful, or guilt-inducing, than telling the truth, and so to reveal itself via the emotional effect on the speaker.

Again, studies of these tells are usually based on the fairly artificial situation of two strangers communicating in a laboratory setting, with not much at stake. But the most reliable clue seems to be that liars include less detail in their stories than do truth-tellers; moreover, liars' stories were sometimes less internally coherent or plausible than the truth (though truth can sometimes be stranger than fiction). Picking up on these clues requires listeners to attend to what's actually said – contrary to what we might have expected, eye contact ('gaze aversion') doesn't bear any relation to lying, nor does um-ing and ah-ing, fidgeting, or scratching.

1. Poker game

Much depends upon what's at stake: where studies required people to lie about matters close to their hearts, they gave away more clues to their lying. This makes sense: everyday 'white lies' are told without a second thought, and are hardly guilt-inducing for most of us, so are unlikely to take an emotional toll. More significant lies may be harder to manage smoothly, and harder to disguise. But the trouble is that telling the truth about matters close to our hearts can also be stressful, and is likely to induce signs easily mistaken for deception cues. If you're speaking about something that is important to you, you may appear dishonest even when you're entirely sincere.

Defaults and track records

It's all terribly complicated. But it's not a hopeless case – we aim with our trusting to identify honest informants, and in real life we have much more to go on than just the internal coherence of what's said, and the accompanying body language. Sometimes, we simply find ourselves trusting or distrusting, without considering whether or why. Other times, trust feels like a conscious decision we have to make, occasionally an agonizing decision. We have responsibility to ourselves and to others to take at least some account of the available evidence, but what policy should we adopt?

One policy is to trust only where we have good evidence that someone is trustworthy. This cautious policy sets the default to distrust: guilty until proven innocent. Taken to its extreme, this policy would make us suspicious of everyone except our close friends and family, where we have had enough opportunity to gather evidence of their honesty – even then we might still be undecided. A less extreme but still cautious policy would concede that our past experience of ticket inspectors is good evidence that we can trust what the ticket inspector says about the train times even when we're in an unfamiliar station, and have never come across this particular inspector before. A different policy sets the default to trust: we should trust people until we have some good reason to think they are untrustworthy. In other words: innocent until proven guilty.

Historically, these rival policies are associated with two great Scottish philosophers – David Hume of Edinburgh, and Thomas Reid of Aberdeen. For Hume, self-sufficiency was of the utmost importance: you must take responsibility for your own beliefs, and accept the word of others only when you have good reason to do so, reason based on your own past experience. Otherwise, you are prone to gullibility, and demagogues. For Hume, an innocent-until-proven-guilty policy is a recipe for disaster, and an irresponsible abdication of duty.

For Reid, trusting what others say is much like trusting our own senses. If we start to doubt the evidence of our senses, we do not have any more basic evidence against which to check what we see and hear. The best we can do is to check one sense against one another – to reach out and touch what we see, or look for the source of a sound. Similarly, argues Reid, if we start to doubt what people say to us, there are limits to the checks we can do. Suppose you begin to get suspicious about what an acquaintance tells you. You can check what he says against reference books, the internet, against what other people say, and so on. But only in a few circumstances can you check out what he says with your own eyes and ears. According to Reid, a blanket guilty-until-proven-innocent policy would mean we never even get started with trusting what others say.

Followers of Reid have argued that a default attitude of trust is necessary for language learning. If we could not simply assume that people's speech generally reflects the way things really are, then we could not begin to associate words with their meanings, and communication would stall. Imagine trying to learn a new language from someone you suspect of being a pathological liar – this would make a difficult task impossible.

When philosophers get caught up in this debate, they are often concerned with trust as a whole – how can we ever be justified in trusting anyone to do or say anything? In everyday life, we do not face this very general question; instead, we face more specific questions about who we can trust to do what, and when. Whether we lean towards Hume or towards Reid, in practical situations we will need to think about context, and about what's at stake. Can you trust the newspaper's claim that the weather will be sunny all week? Yes, if you're just trying to decide whether to hang out the washing to dry. No, if you're deciding whether to take out insurance for an expensive outdoor wedding. Can you trust your neighbour to look after your pet when you're on holiday? Yes, if it's a goldfish that needs feeding once a week. No, if it's a Great Dane that needs a special diet and twice-daily walks. When the stakes are low, we don't need much evidence; when there's more at stake, we need more. In particular, when we hold responsibility for making trust decisions that affect third parties, we may need to set the threshold higher.

Dan Sperber and his co-workers have investigated our reactions to trust situations, trying to establish whether we have a default of trust, or of distrust. As Reid argued, default distrust is just too demanding – in many situations, the stakes are low, lies seem fairly infrequent, and the costs in time and energy of searching for evidence of trustworthiness are not worth the reward of avoiding occasional deceptions. But we need to be sensitive to changes in the stakes, the environment, and the plausibility of what we're told – 'epistemic vigilance' is key. Sperber draws an analogy with the vigilance we exercise in walking down a crowded street. In general, we expect others to avoid bumping into us, and do not constantly calculate others' trajectories. But we pursue low-level, even unconscious, monitoring of other people's behaviour, in a way which can rise to consciousness when it seems that something is about to go wrong. Vigilance underpins trust, on this picture.

The Nyāya tradition in Indian philosophy, which traces its roots back over two thousand years, offers an account of trust that prefigures Sperber's. Like Reid, Nyāya thinkers point to the impossibility of assessing each speaker's credentials before accepting their words: we are entitled to directly accept unless we know of some reason to doubt. As with Sperber, the idea of unconscious monitoring is key: we are alert to possible problems without having to consciously review the evidence and laboriously draw a conclusion on every occasion. You don't have to ponder everything, so long as you are primed to notice inconsistencies or errors.

The habit of epistemic vigilance is acquired young, but not extremely young. Children below the age of four find it difficult to grasp the idea of deliberate deception or even the idea that different people have different views about the world. Learning when to be suspicious, and when to accept what you're told, requires a number of different cognitive mechanisms, which can develop at different rates, and in different ways for different children. What generates these differences? Atsushi Sakai studied pairs of identical and non-identical twins in Japan, along with non-twin siblings, investigating the level of trust they place in friends and family members, and the degree to which they feel trusted in return. He found that aspects of the environment explained attitudes of trust, and feelings of being trusted, with no need to posit any genetic variation. This doesn't tell us exactly which aspects of our environment are key, but it does dispel the idea that some of us are just born to trust, and others born to be suspicious.

Whatever our environment, as we get older, we rely more and more upon social facts about reputation, for better or for worse, and so it becomes crucial to look more closely at how reputations are created and maintained.

Gentlemen and good repute

In 17th-century England, some were gentlemen, and some were not. Being gentle required the right combination of wealth, birth, and character, but there was little agreement about which of these three was fundamental. Money alone wasn't enough – the old problem of the *nouveau riche* – yet poverty made it impossible to maintain basic standards of gentlemanly living and decorum. Being born to a 'good' family clearly mattered, though a country squire could be just as much a gentleman as the grand old Duke of York; indeed, the political entanglements of those at the very top of society could make it hard for them to behave like proper gentlemen.

Such proper gentlemanly behaviour was the outward sign of inward virtue, though rival traditions valued different sorts of virtue. A chivalric tradition prioritized honour, dignity, and physical courage, but these traits were in tension with the Christian virtues of meekness, humility, and self-control, which underpinned a life pursued with an eye to God's final judgement rather than to worldly reputation.

Whatever makes him so, a gentleman's word is his bond. He can be trusted to tell the truth, unlike his unreliable inferiors. He has credibility in the courtroom, as witness or juror, he has credibility in scientific contexts, as reporter of natural occurrences or experimental findings, and he has credibility in everyday life. Labourers, servants, and, for the most part, women, cannot be trusted to speak the truth. To modern ears, this sounds like a nasty bit of class and gender prejudice.

But within the social structures of the time, ideas about gentlemanly wealth, birth, and character combined to furnish explanations of gentlemanly truth-telling. Wealth is the key to freedom, for the gentleman is not obliged to work for others – he has independent means, and so is free to speak the truth as he finds it. He is creditworthy in every sense. Servants or wives, in contrast, cannot speak independently of the employers or husbands upon whom they depend; likewise, tradesmen and merchants cannot afford to speak the truth if this is bad for business.

Honesty was part of honour, so to indulge in dishonesty was to run the risk of being dishonoured, whereas the lower orders have no honour in the first place, so have less motive to tell the truth where this is inconvenient. Indeed, to question a gentleman's honesty was to question his very status as gentleman, and an accusation of lying was a grave insult, one that became semi-formalized in the culture of duelling. It was better to be challenged than challenger, for the challenged party was allowed to choose the weapons. So if trouble was brewing, each gentleman would try to manoeuvre the other into issuing the challenge. 'Giving the lie' – accusing someone of dishonesty – was the ultimate insult, and so forced out the challenge. Pistols at dawn!

Some explanations of gentlemanly reliability reflect upon motives: who has a motive to lie, who a motive to speak the truth? What are the penalties for being discovered in a lie; what troubles may be caused by speaking the truth? Though our own social and epistemic categories are different from those of 17th-century England, we too may consider motive and consequences in deciding who to believe, who to trust. This is why, in public life, people are often required to declare conflicts of interest, to display their potential motives for others to consider.

For example, the UK Houses of Parliament publishes registers of members' interests. Why?: '...to provide information on any financial or non-financial benefit received by a MP or Member of the Lords which might reasonably be thought by others to influence their actions, speeches or votes in Parliament...'. Members are not forbidden from voting or speaking about matters where they have an interest, but the register is supposed to provide the rest of us with some context by which to judge their likely trustworthiness in such circumstances. Motive, motive, motive.

Yet the concepts of honour and insult, still with us today, seem to reflect more upon character than on motive. If I openly weigh up what motives my husband may have to lie to me, what troubles he may incur by speaking the truth, then this already indicates a diminution of my trust in him, and he could fairly take offence; all this even if, on balance, I decide it is reasonable to believe what he says. Instead, my husband wants me simply to see that he wouldn't lie to me, because of the relationship we have, and because of his moral character. Lying is just not the sort of thing he would do. Likewise, the gentleman is not just someone who happens to be in a situation where the rewards for telling the truth usually outweigh the rewards for lying; he is supposed to be someone who is naturally, instinctively disposed to speak the truth, someone who finds it painful to lie.

In judging honesty, then, we try to judge both character and circumstance, and the balance between these may differ according to how well we know the person in question. When I trust a stranger for directions on the street, I know nothing of his character. But I do know that there is little to be gained by lying in such circumstances; matters might be different if I'm asking the stranger to recommend a shop or café, in an area where he may have a personal stake in a local business.

Partiality and prejudice

In thinking about trust, it's easy to focus on interactions amongst strangers or, at best, acquaintances. How do we judge one another?; how should we judge one another?; do we need to judge one another? But many issues about trust – or distrust – arise within the context of a relationship, amongst family members, friends, lovers, colleagues, or neighbours. How does increased intimacy change what we should do? And how do personal considerations weigh in the balance alongside cold hard fact?

In close friendships, we feel inclined, even obligated, to offer the benefit of the doubt, to assume that our friends are being honest with us, unless we have clear evidence to the contrary. Is this because friendship itself is a reason to trust? Perhaps, but it's also true that we have amassed a great deal of positive evidence about those we know well. The reason you should trust your friend even when she is accused of shoplifting is that you have known her for years, and therefore have very good evidence that she has not done what she is accused of doing. But is this evidence all that counts? When we start to calculate the odds in deciding whether to trust our friends or family, they may rightly resent us.

Philosophers Sarah Stroud and Simon Keller argue that part of friendship is the commitment to put a positive spin on the picture you have of your friends: to defend them to others, to resist believing malicious gossip about them, and to assume that they are behaving from good motives, even when you can't quite see what these are. There are limits, of course, but pushing up against these limits can be painful for both parties: when does the evidence force you to concede that the worst may be true? When we see the mothers or wives of criminals stand by their man, we may pity them, but it's hard to condemn. Rationality doesn't require us to ignore our human relationships.

Trusting can also be a way of building trustworthiness – people have little incentive to speak the truth if they know they will be assumed to be lying in any case – and perhaps we have a special obligation to help our loved ones develop their trustworthiness in these ways. Other relationships of responsibility or care can also bring obligations like this: teaching essentially involves an extension of trust, and part of the intended effects of such trust is an increase in the trustworthiness of the student, both in terms of their knowledge, and in terms of intellectual openness.

There is a darker side to these personal considerations, however. How far can I extend the benefit of the doubt which I give to my close friends? What if I trust people I grew up with, and no-one else? What if I don't trust anybody over the age of 30, as Jack Weinberg urged student protesters at Berkeley during the 1960s? What if I don't trust Japanese people because of my nasty prejudices about wily Orientals?

Getting it right about trust is a good thing for us as trusters – enabling us to take advantage of positive collaborations, and avoid being taken for a ride – but it is also important for those on the receiving end, the trustees (or distrustees, if they're unlucky). When dealing with our friends, we may allow friendship to weigh in the balance, to tip us towards trust rather than distrust. But this doesn't license us to use other, less pleasant, personal feelings to deny someone our trust where the evidence doesn't demand this.

Some controversial studies have suggested that people living in more ethnically diverse neighbourhoods are likely to report lower levels of generalized trust. But levels of trust increase when people actually interact with their neighbours, engaging with them as individuals rather than anonymous members of a racial group. These studies are hard to interpret, however, since ethnically diverse neighbourhoods are often also economically deprived neighbourhoods, which in turn are often low-trust environments because of everyday experiences with crime, disorder, and transience. It can be quite reasonable, even essential, to exercise severe caution in such circumstances.

All of us are prone to biases even if we don't realize it, and even if we consciously reject sexist or racist attitudes. Project Implicit, at Harvard University, has run more than 4.5 million tests, each aimed to probe the subject's associations between, for example, black or white faces and negative or positive imagery. Other variants contrast young or old faces, thin or fat, male or female, and so on. Over and over again, people are quicker to associate black faces with negative images, and white with positive: strikingly, this is true even for black people who take the test, and even for people of whatever ethnicity who sincerely disown these associations. If you think you will be the exception, I encourage you to give it a try on the Project Implicit website.

Sadly, being well-meaning isn't enough. Even concentrating on the possibility of bias, sternly telling yourself not to be prejudiced, can have a counter-productive effect, perhaps because the mental effort involved in concentrating on this point actually makes it harder to resist the stereotypes once you let your guard down. But what is more effective is imagining, or, better still, interacting with people from the stereotyped group who do not fit the stereotype. This is one way to understand the importance of role models: female car mechanics, active octogenarians, and black presidents. The more we think about, and encounter, people who don't fit the stereotypical mould, the easier it is for us to resist our unconscious prejudices. This fits with the studies of ethnically diverse neighbourhoods: people felt more trusting when they actually got out and engaged with their neighbours as individuals, rather than viewing them through the net curtains as members of a homogeneous group. These measures can help us judge other people – and their honesty in particular – on their merits, without relying on stereotypes we consciously reject.

Chapter 6
Knowledge and expertise

Honesty and good intentions are not enough: in trusting, we also seek competence. If I trust what you tell me about where to find a reliable builder, I trust that you are honest, but I must also trust that you know what you're talking about. If I trust you to look after my pets when I'm on holiday, I trust that your intentions are good, but I must also trust that you know how to look after a Great Dane and a Siberian hamster.

The knowledge aspect of trust is often less morally fraught than the honesty aspect of trust. Discussions of the 'crisis of trust', in politics or elsewhere, usually focus on doubts about honesty, or good intentions, rather than doubts about skill or knowledge – we might worry about the (in)competency of our politicians, but are less likely to express these worries in terms of trust. After all, someone who makes an honest mistake is more readily forgiven than someone who deliberately deceives us or knowingly lets us down. But such tolerance has its limits, and those who assume positions of responsibility are obliged to maintain the requisite levels of expertise.

Estelle Morris resigned from her position as UK Minister for Education in 2002, saying that she did not have the right skills for the job, and that 'second-best' was not good enough for such a crucial role. Her resignation followed a sequence of crises and problems, but nevertheless she was widely applauded for her honesty and integrity. If we can trust what she said about her reasons for resigning (and that's a further question), Morris was displaying impressive trustworthiness: recognizing that she was not able to meet the commitments of her job, she stepped down from the job, rather than live with unmet commitments.

Does trustworthiness always require expertise? Not necessarily. We can be trustworthy in areas where we know little, so long as we know our limits. If you don't know how to cure cancer, that by itself doesn't make you untrustworthy. But if you don't know how to cure cancer, yet you confidently start dispensing advice about this, then you make yourself untrustworthy. Likewise with pet care: you can be trustworthy even without knowing what hamsters like to eat. But you shouldn't offer to take care of any hamsters unless you know what they like to eat (or can readily find out).

Trustworthiness is a matter of meeting commitments, and this requires both good intentions and competence. Part of being trustworthy is trying to avoid commitments you are not competent to fulfil, as well as trying to fulfil the commitments you already have. It's an awful feeling, being trapped with a commitment you know you can't live up to, especially when the stakes are high, and others are depending upon you. Such experiences can – or should – make us think twice about the promises we make in the future.

This means that self-knowledge is also required for trustworthiness. Being honest with ourselves about what we know, and what we don't, about our capacities, skills, and weaknesses, is a pre-requisite for being trustworthy to other people. And when, in our turn, we're looking for people to trust, we should be looking for people who know their own strengths, and also know their own limits. Trustworthy people are often good at assessing their own skills, knowledge, and limitations, so that they know when to offer help

Knowledge and expertise

or advice and when to stand back. Sometimes, the trustworthy option is to say 'I don't know', or 'I'm afraid I can't do that for you', even when we know this will disappoint. To be trustworthy to others, we need to be honest with ourselves about what we can realistically manage, and where our weaknesses lie. Over-optimism about our own talents gives rise to one form of untrustworthiness.

This kind of self-knowledge is not always easily obtained. Sometimes we can measure our skills and knowledge by external standards, entering competitions or passing exams. But often this isn't feasible, and we may be prone to over- or under-estimating ourselves, depending upon our levels of confidence, or even arrogance. Moreover, this kind of self-knowledge can sometimes require excessive navel-gazing. Achieving accurate, detailed estimation of my own talents and expertise is hardly the noblest goal I can set myself in life.

But these problems about self-knowledge help explain why complete trustworthiness is difficult to achieve, as it certainly is. It can be difficult to know what we're capable of, and therefore difficult to know what we ought to offer to other people. Am I really able to fulfil the demands of this new job?; am I really in a position to offer financial advice?; am I really so certain of my opinions that I should seek to influence others? Betrayals of trust that arise from mistakes about such matters may be more forgivable than intentional betrayals that arise from dishonesty, but they are failures of trustworthiness nonetheless.

The distinction between competence or skill, on the one hand, and honesty or good intentions, on the other, is clear enough in principle, but it can be blurred in practice. Long experience has taught me not to trust my friend Daisy to show up on time when we agree to meet. I'll arrange to meet somewhere I don't mind waiting alone, take a book, or show up late myself. But what's Daisy's problem? Is it that she can't turn up on time, or that she

66

can't be bothered? Incompetence, or lack of good intentions? It's probably a bit of both: she doesn't find it easy to be punctual, but she's not exactly doing her utmost to overcome this difficulty.

The same goes for trusting what people say. I can't trust what Maisie tells me about her son's glittering career. She isn't deliberately lying to me, but she is allowing herself to believe her son is a great success, despite all the evidence which points in the opposite direction, and she's passing on this shaky belief to me as straightforward fact. Is she dishonest? Not entirely: she believes what she says. But nor is she simply making an innocent error: she's in a position to know better. Again, both honesty and knowledge are in question, and it's hard to draw a sharp line between them.

Nevertheless, investigations of trust often focus on one aspect to the exclusion of the other. The 'trust game' experiments, in which people decide whether to hand over money to another person, in the hopes of getting an increased return, seem focused on good intentions rather than competence. Given the set-up, it is obvious that the recipient is *capable* of returning some money, so the only question is whether they *will*. (The fact that honesty is not at stake here confirms that the trust games test only one aspect of trusting behaviour.) Chimpanzees seem to have reciprocal arrangements to exchange food and grooming, and it is usually obvious to all concerned whether these resources are available at a given time; the only uncertainty regards intentions. Likewise, the experiments on deception detection, body language, and tells are of course directed at our judgements about others' honesty, not their level of knowledge.

To think about the competence aspect of trust – and trustworthiness – we need to think about how we get knowledge from what other people say, and about how we identify skilled practitioners, people with know-how.

Who knows?

We're in a tricky position when we lack knowledge and turn to others for help. How can I tell who has the knowledge I need? I can't just quiz people to check whether they have the right answers – if I knew what the right answers were, I wouldn't need their help in the first place. When we're looking for skills, rather than straightforward factual knowledge, life is sometimes a little easier: I can tell that my mother knows how to drive, even though I don't know how to drive myself, because I'm sitting in the passenger seat watching her drive. But not all skills are so easily assessed: I don't know how to speak Gujarati, and I can't tell whether the couple in front of me on the bus know how to speak Gujarati. I know they're chatting in a language I don't recognize, but that's as far as I can get.

So how do we spot knowers? One clue is status or prestige. When UK newspapers want commentary on a scientific issue, they often turn to Martin Rees. I'm guessing he's Martin to his friends, but to the rest of us he is Professor Martin Rees, Baron Rees of Ludlow, member of the Order of Merit, Master of Trinity College Cambridge, Astronomer Royal, former President of the Royal Society, Reith lecturer, and winner of a dozen high-profile prizes for scientific research and communication. He even has an asteroid named after him. Most of us are not in a position to check Lord Rees's scientific expertise at first hand, but his long list of credentials make him an obviously excellent source of information about astrophysics.

Many of these credentials give us a kind of second- or third-hand assurance about Rees's expertise. After all, membership of the Order of Merit is in the personal gift of the Queen, whilst both the Astronomer Royal and the Master of Trinity are appointed by the Queen on the advice of the Prime Minister. Has Elizabeth simply taken a shine to Martin? After all, our Queen is not known for her astrophysical expertise, and nor are our recent Prime Ministers. But if we take these credentials seriously, it is because we assume that the Queen takes advice from the PM, who takes advice from his officials, who in turn take advice from scientists who themselves have strong credentials in the relevant field. Rees's long list of awards reflects the high esteem in which he is held by others who are held in high esteem in their mutual profession. Likewise, the hundreds of publications he has in peer-reviewed academic journals reflect the fact that his research has been highly rated by other experts in his field. If Martin Rees tells me something about black holes, I'll believe him.

In recent years, Rees has written more widely about science beyond astrophysics, and about the future of human civilization, climate change, alien life forms, and other exciting topics, always in an accessible way which rewards the reader's attention. In his 2010 Reith lectures, he even addressed issues about science, credentials, trust, and the media. But how far do Rees's credentials as an astrophysicist stretch to cover these more general topics? We can be certain that he is a highly intelligent man, with all sorts of resources to call upon, but there is a danger in simply transferring credentials from one field to another. Interviewed in the *Independent* newspaper (27th September 2010), Rees rejected his friend Stephen Hawking's view that humans would inevitably colonize space – 'I think that's an ill-thought-through statement' – and Hawking's view that cosmology makes God redundant:

> Stephen Hawking is a remarkable person whom I've known for 40 years, and for that reason any oracular statement he makes gets exaggerated publicity. I know Stephen Hawking well enough to know that he has read very little philosophy and even less theology, so I don't think we should attach any weight to his views on this topic.

Rees and Hawking are extreme cases, credentials-wise, but everyone has a reputation, good or bad, and some people have formal qualifications, certificates, and letters after their names. When we look for others with knowledge or skill, these reputations and reputational markers can be a useful, if fallible, guide.

Another clue is provided by access. Sometimes we can see that other people are in a position to know things that we don't. If I see you're reading the TV schedule in the newspaper, I'll ask you what's on tonight. 'Sources close to' the prime minister are regarded as likely to know what's going on at the top, as are the ubiquitous 'friends' of Jen, Brad, and Angelina who are quoted in celebrity magazines. Eye-witnesses are important in court cases, because they are assumed to have special knowledge of what occurred, whilst hearsay evidence is taken to be less reliable.

Different clues are provided by track records. Some sources have a history of just getting things right, even though we don't know how they come by their information or skills, and perhaps would prefer not to know. And of course, these different sorts of clues can work together: a track record of getting things right may be reflected by informal or formal credentials and reputation.

Social psychologists have studied what they call the 'expertise heuristic', often because they're interested in the power of advertising messages. When we're deciding whether to believe what someone says, we assess the speaker as well as assessing the inherent plausibility of what's said. Details such as a speaker's occupation or experience naturally affect the audience's willingness to believe what's said. But so does the speed at which someone talks. In general, the faster someone speaks, the more competent and knowledgeable they appear to be. In part, this is because fast speakers appear more confident, but fast speech also makes it harder for the audience to spot any weaknesses in the argument or evidence being presented. (It is, however, possible to speak too quickly: if a speaker tips over into near-incomprehensibility, then this undermines the audience's confidence in what she's saying.)

Length and detail also add to persuasiveness (which is somewhat unfortunate for the author of a *Very Short Introduction*). It's perhaps not surprising that greater detail creates an impression of expertise, but even speaking for longer in a repetitive or fairly empty way can create a superficial impression of expertise, though this can be dispelled in situations where the audience has a lot at stake, and is paying more careful attention.

Making these snap judgements isn't always a bad thing. In many everyday situations, we are not at significant risk of error, and the stakes are fairly low. The opportunity cost of taking our time to carefully evaluate every message we receive, every speaker who offers us information, might lead to a small increase in accuracy, but at the price of a large decrease in efficiency. Heuristics help us get through life, but they are not always a useful guide as to who to trust in more weighty matters.

Experts in society

Should you get your child injected with the MMR triple-vaccine? Are human actions significantly affecting the climate? Can onshore wind farms make a useful contribution to our energy needs? Was bad parenting the main cause of rioting in UK cities in August 2011? Does prison work? Well, I know what I think, and you probably have strong views about at least some of these issues yourself. But neither of us is an expert about all of these complex matters, and in forming our views we have relied in part, carefully or carelessly, on the alleged views of alleged experts.

Given the complexity of our society, and the technologies we live with, expert advice is essential. One traditional picture is that experts should provide factual information about different options and possibilities, without any injection of their personal values. It is for society as a whole, via the usual democratic processes, to decide which values to enact. So, for example, experts may give us information about the consequences of various custodial and noncustodial punishment regimes for re-offending rates. But these experts do not have a special role in deciding whether our justice system should prioritize the avoidance of re-offending, or moral retribution, or the wishes of victims, or the individual rights of criminals, or financial efficiency. On this traditional picture, facts and values can be kept quite separate, and the only issue is making sure that experts are honest enough to keep their personal prejudices out of their science.

There are many difficulties with this traditional picture. People can and do disagree about which questions need expert input, and what kind of expertise is relevant. Does bad parenting cause riots? Social scientists see this as a tricky long-term question, unlikely to have a 'yes-or-no' answer, and requiring careful data collection and complex statistical methods. Many newspaper columnists, politicians, and members of the public instead see this as a matter of common sense: surely it's obvious that good parents don't let their teenagers out at night when there are riots going on, and surely it's obvious that good parents instil decent moral values in their kids, values that include not breaking shop windows and looting consumer goods. Here, there is disagreement about whether expertise is necessary, and about whether having kids of your own, or living in the affected areas, gives you a kind of expertise in these matters, even if that's not recognized by a formal qualification.

In other matters, such as wind farms, it is uncontroversial that some technical expertise is required to help answer the question. How do wind turbines work? How much energy can they produce under various weather conditions? How much noise do they create, and what effect do they have on birds or other wildlife? These sound like purely factual questions which can be settled by scientific enquiry before we go on to the 'value questions' about how to trade off local concerns against national demands, aesthetics against practicalities, or current problems against the fate of future generations. But those who disagree about whether we should be building wind farms tend to disagree about the factual questions too: there is no universally acknowledged expert source of information about these matters that will allow us to proceed smoothly to contemplation of the value questions.

Sometimes there is genuine and widespread disagreement amongst the experts on a given topic. Other times, there is near-consensus, but this fact can be disguised by press coverage that values controversy or apparent balance. In 2011, Professor Steve Jones – expert geneticist, science communicator, and another Reith lecturer – was commissioned to review the BBC's science coverage, supported by the Science Communication Unit at University College London. BBC editorial guidelines require due impartiality, but Jones concluded that scrupulous efforts to meet this requirement often meant that the opinions of a small minority were given more weight and exposure than they merited, making issues seem contentious when in fact they were not.

Editors and journalists have a difficult line to tread; even when they have a scientific training, they cannot be experts in all the many sub-fields of the natural and social sciences which may sometimes hit the headlines. Falling in line with apparent consensus can mean that important dissenting views go unheard, but giving airtime to all the dissenters can misrepresent the state of expert opinion.

What are we, as citizens, to make of all this? Who can we believe? Perhaps the solution lies in increased public understanding of science. On the 'deficit model' of public understanding, it is the duty of scientists to transmit what they can of their specialized knowledge to the public, who have a deficit of such knowledge; this will enable ordinary people to understand scientific issues and controversies more clearly. Whilst increased scientific knowledge is a great aspiration, it's unlikely that most of us can really put ourselves in a position to evaluate scientific controversies for ourselves, judging which side has the upper hand. Indeed, contemporary science is so huge and diverse that individual scientists themselves can evaluate controversies only in the relatively small area of their own expertise, and must approach other parts of science as outsiders.

A rival picture of public understanding places more emphasis on our understanding of how science works as a social institution: how controversies are settled, who gets to publish what and where, what is the difference between speculation, theory, and evidence, and what sorts of pressures scientists work under. In particular, the state of knowledge, dissent, and consensus may vary significantly between different areas of science, especially when we include social sciences such as economics. In 2003, the *Independent* newspaper reported the chairman of HSBC boasting that Household International, a company recently acquired by HSBC, had 150 PhD-educated experts evaluating the risks involved in their business. Household specialized in offering sub-prime mortgages, and its subsequent troubles led to HSBC's needing UK government bailout by 2008. Consensus amongst the experts in this case turned out to be a massive mistake.

A grasp of the mechanics of science, and social science, should help us get a better grip on the nature and significance of disagreement and consensus amongst different sorts of experts – this cannot replace trust, but will help us place our trust wisely.

Finally, we need to be alert to knowledge and expertise that arise from situation and experience, not just from formal education and training. Sociologist Brian Wynne studied the impact of the 1986 Chernobyl nuclear disaster on sheep farming in the hills of England's Lake District. At issue were the short-term and long-term effects of radioactivity on the sheep that grazed the hills, and the consequences for the farmers' ability to sell their sheep at market. Immediately after the event, official pronouncements downplayed the likely effects, but in subsequent weeks, more and more radioactivity was detected on the hills, and in the sheep. Restrictions on sale were extended, significantly damaging the farmers' already precarious livelihoods, just as the farmers had warned. The farmers had long experience of the effects of radioactivity on their stock, because of a sequence of incidents at the local nuclear plant, Windscale (renamed 'Sellafield' after a particularly nasty accident), and were able to apply this experience to the Chernobyl situation. Wynne concluded that the farmers' own 'lay' expertise was in many respects deeper and more accurate than that of the scientists. Alongside public understanding of science, we need mutual engagement between scientists and nonscientists.

Self-trust

Trust is most commonly discussed as it arises between different people – or between people and institutions – and this book fits that pattern too. But sometimes when I ask 'who should I trust?', one good answer is 'myself'. And sometimes I really ought to distrust myself, whether or not I can bring myself to do so.

Issues about self-trust are likely to come up only when there is some challenge to this trust. Can I trust myself not to get angry when I confront my noisy neighbour? Can I trust myself to buy all the groceries we need if I don't make a list? Can I trust myself not to smoke if there are cigarettes in the house? These are questions about what I can trust myself to do, but there are also questions of self-trust in connection with knowledge and evidence: can I trust what I think I remember, or could I be fooling myself? Can I trust my instinctive judgement about a situation or person, or might my prejudices or hopes be leading me astray?

Self-trust is both like and unlike the full-blown moralized trust we sometimes invest in other people, the kind of trust on which intimate relationships can be founded, and which leads to feelings of resentment and betrayal when it goes wrong. Sometimes, self-trust seems to involve a divided self, a contrast between the 'me' who must decide whether to trust, and the 'me' who is the target of the trust – often in the past or the future. The current me is not tempted to smoke, but can I trust the later version of me who has had a glass of wine, or should I instead take precautions to remove any temptations from later me? This divided self picture prods us towards treating self-trust as a special case of trusting others, thinking of our earlier and later selves as especially intimate 'others'.

Does self-trust carry the same moral weight as trust in others? After all, if I trust myself, but this turns out to be a mistake, I may feel frustrated and disappointed, but it would be unusual to think that I have betrayed myself, and stranger still to demand an apology of myself. In typical interpersonal cases, inviting someone's trust and then disappointing them is regarded as a moral failing, an untrustworthiness that merits disapproval. But my later self doesn't exactly invite the trust of my earlier self, nor make binding promises. There is a lot to be gained from being strong-willed, able to make good your earlier intentions; for example, it would be tough to quit smoking without this kind of will-power. But this kind of determination is somewhat different from the kind of commitment to others that is required for promise-keeping and trustworthiness.

Philosopher Carolyn McLeod develops other links between self-trust and ethics. She argues that appropriate self-trust is an important element of autonomy – the ability to think, act, and choose for ourselves – and that this can be especially significant when we need to make decisions about healthcare in the context of modern medicine. It becomes difficult to trust ourselves if others do not trust us, or if others tell us we are untrustworthy in some domain, because we do not have the requisite specialist knowledge. Promoting and protecting patients' self-trust is a key part of respecting their autonomy. Indeed, a degree of self-trust comes into our decisions about trusting others: can I trust myself to know who to trust?

As with trust in others, our decisions to trust ourselves must be guided, although perhaps not fully determined, by the evidence available. Experience has taught me that I can't be trusted to watch just one episode of *30 Rock*, then switch off and get back to writing this book; if I want to get more writing done, then I shouldn't start watching the DVD in the first place. Experience has also told me that I have a bad memory for colours; if I want shoes to match this dress, I can't trust myself to make the right choice unless I take the dress along to the shoe shop.

Sometimes it's good to let our self-trust outrun the evidence a little, if improved self-trust and self-confidence can actually improve our performance. Just as trusting other people can make them more trustworthy, under the right circumstances at least, trusting ourselves can make ourselves more capable, more successful, even more trustworthy. But, as with trusting others, we need to be careful about outrunning the evidence if other people's vital interests are at stake. Inspirational slogans about self-confidence do not license my believing I'm perfectly able to drive a 57-seat bus without training. And if I believe I can fly, things won't end well, no matter how uplifted I feel.

We have some responsibility to help those around us achieve a sensible level of self-awareness and self-trust, both in medical contexts, as McLeod argues, and elsewhere. Indeed, one damaging effect of verbal abuse and insults can be a downgrading of the victim's self-trust; domestic abuse can reduce the victim's self-trust to the extent that it becomes difficult for victims to trust themselves either to judge the reality of the situation, or to find a way out. More positively, an important role for teachers and coaches is to enable students to earn and establish self-trust in their areas of expertise. And as parents, we take on the delicate task of inculcating both self-confidence and self-awareness in our children, whilst knowing that we likely do – even should – overestimate the talents of our own little darlings.

Choice and responsibility

Trusting or distrusting doesn't always feel like something we choose to do – very often, we simply find ourselves in a state of trust or distrust, with little awareness of how we have arrived there. So what's the point of thinking about who we should trust, if trusting lies beyond our control?

Just as we can find ourselves trusting (or distrusting), we find ourselves believing or not, with little sense of control. I believe that Margaret Thatcher was the first female prime minister of the UK, that cruelty is wrong, and that I will never meet Clint Eastwood. I think that each of these beliefs is reasonable, though I might find it difficult to pinpoint exactly the evidence I have in their favour. Moreover, I cannot simply abandon these beliefs at will, not even if you offer me a large bribe to do so. If you want me to change my mind, you will have to produce – or fabricate – some evidence against these beliefs, perhaps a newspaper report that Eastwood will be visiting my workplace next week, or that Churchill was in fact a woman. In the latter case, it will take more than a single report to change my mind, and it is hard for me to imagine what sort of evidence could possibly change my mind about the wrongness of cruelty, even if it would be convenient for me to change my mind.

Trusting someone to do something is often a matter of believing they are trustworthy in the relevant respect. When trust involves belief, it is no surprise that it lies beyond our direct control: I cannot simply decide to believe you are trustworthy. Even when I trust you without fully believing you to be trustworthy, my evidence places some constraints on my trust. If I firmly believed you were totally untrustworthy, it's hard to see how I could trust you in any respect. I might be able to pretend to trust you, to behave in public as if I trust you. But actual trust would be beyond my reach.

Nevertheless, the fact that we do not in general choose our beliefs, or choose who to trust, does not mean that our beliefs and trust are beyond evaluation. This is harder to see in our own first-personal situations, but when we look at those around us, it's not difficult to see examples of reasonable and unreasonable beliefs. Here, reasonableness is not just a matter of truth: I can disagree with what my friend believes without thinking she is being unreasonable, perhaps because I have access to better evidence than she does. I can see that, given her situation, she has drawn the only sensible conclusion, but I also know that she is wrong about the facts.

So even where trust and belief go hand in hand, and go beyond our direct choice, they are still liable to assessments of reasonableness and unreasonableness. And we can all do our best to make the right judgements about trust and distrust, about honesty and dishonesty.

Philosopher Miranda Fricker has emphasized the moral and political importance of ensuring that people get a fair hearing; she argues that we can do significant harm to others when our prejudices – about race, class, or gender, for example – reduce the trust we place in them. Such prejudices can lead to expectations of deceit, as with 'feminine wiles', or to expectations of ignorance, as with 'foolish girls'. Expectations of deceit may carry more moral condemnation than expectations of ignorance, but both can lead to effective silencing of disadvantaged groups. It's easy to see how this can be practically damaging – if you don't get your voice heard, your interests are likely be overlooked. But Fricker argues that the damage goes deeper – if you don't get your voice heard, if you don't get to express your knowledge, there is an important sense in which it doesn't really count as knowledge. Knowledge is the sort of thing we can share and transmit; unshareable knowledge loses much of its value.

Fricker urges us to 'epistemic justice', due regard for the voices of others, for their sake. But of course, we have much to gain ourselves from listening to others, or at least from judging their trustworthiness by considering the evidence, not by relying upon our prejudices. We damage ourselves if we close our ears to sources of information or cooperation which would otherwise be open to us.

Chapter 7
Trust on the internet

When my twin babies were napping, I would browse online forums for parents – usually mothers – of multiples. Sometimes I'd pick up practical tips, but mostly I just gained consolation from the fact that others were also struggling with exhaustion, or had emerged from the early stages to enjoy life with their toddler twins. It was salutary to see people managing under much harder circumstances than mine – as single parents, with older children to care for too, with financial troubles, with medical issues. And I was in awe of parents of triplets and more, both for their sheer survival and for the mutual support they provided in their area of the forum, where I would lurk occasionally.

It was mostly triplets, and a couple of sets of quads, but one mother had baby triplets *and* toddler twins. Unsurprisingly, her life was tough, all the more so after her partner left, but the other triplet mums were always ready to console, to offer advice, and to try to boost her spirits. One of the triplets became seriously ill, and was hospitalized – imagine the practicalities of coping with that alone – but eventually recovered. Then super-mum decided to emigrate to New Zealand, where her extended family lived, and she detailed the traumas of packing and preparing for such a long flight alone with five tiny children. Finally, she had tripped herself up. Other triplet mums knew from their own experience that airlines insist on one adult passenger to accompany each baby, so the story had to be false. Super-mum was called out as a fake, and (apparently) never returned to the forum.

I was shaken up, but I was only a spectator, who had neither offered my support, nor revealed details of my own life. More active participants seemed devastated, exposed, and at a loss to know how to react, how to regard the time and emotional energy they had invested in the affair, or how to continue the forum. Who else might be fake? How can I find out, without destroying genuine friendships? Who might think I'm a fake? How can I prove I'm not? Soon after, the forum was overhauled to require registration and passwords; I drifted away.

There were fakes and frauds before there was the internet: bigamists, financial cheats, and masters of the art such as Frank Abagnale Jr, played by Leonardo di Caprio in Spielberg's *Catch Me If You Can*. But the internet amplifies and changes what's possible, for better and for worse. Ten years earlier, I would have had little or no contact with other parents of twins, let alone triplets. On the other hand, any contact would have been two-way: I couldn't have hung out and listened without contributing myself. Super-mum would have found it almost impossible to carry out her fraud face to face – it's hard to fake three babies in real life. But perhaps some of the genuine mums would have found it impossible to discuss their problems and feelings offline, to get the support they needed without having to involve others in their lives. Several studies have found that anonymous internet interaction can lead to greater – or quicker – 'self-disclosure' than does face-to-face interaction.

The internet is not a monolith, and the many ways we use the internet raise many different issues about trust; some of these simply extend the issues that arise offline, whilst others are new.

2. Web (in)security

When can you trust what you read on *Wikipedia*? What about 'customer' reviews or recommendations on sites like Amazon, TripAdvisor, or Ebay? Who can you trust with your credit card details? What about online dating sites, and the beaux and belles who inhabit them? What kind of trust is required in Massively Multiplayer Online Role-Playing Games (MMORPGs)? And what do we expect from blogs, forums, or Twitter users, pseudonymous or otherwise? In this chapter, I discuss just three case studies – *Wikipedia*, online dating, and customer reviews.

Wikipedia

The web is a morass of information sources. Some, like the BBC, traditional newspapers, and university- or government-sponsored sites are affiliated with nonvirtual institutions which lend them credibility: our trust in these sites is supported by knowing who lies behind them, knowing their track record, and knowing the incentives they have to get things right. Others have no identifiable connections to nonvirtual institutions, but have nevertheless developed a reputation for accuracy, a reputation worth preserving.

Wikipedia is something else entirely. English-language *Wikipedia* contains nearly four million articles, each of which can be edited by any of the four hundred million different people who visit the site each month. That it exists at all is a remarkable testament to what people are willing to do unpaid and, for the most part, unacknowledged. No qualifications or expertise are required to join in, no entry has an identifiable single author, and there is no editor who takes overall responsibility for the accuracy of what's published. It's impossible to make a sweeping judgement about whether or not we should 'trust *Wikipedia*', any more than we can decide whether or not to 'trust books' or 'trust what people say'; we may begin with a default attitude of moderate trust, or tempered scepticism, but this won't guide us far.

Instead, we need to think about how to assess individual articles, just as we assess individual books or people for likely honesty and accuracy. In assessing more traditional sources, we can consider reputation, credentials, and track record; we can consider the inherent plausibility of what's said, and its coherence with what we already know; we can consider whether the author or speaker is in a position to know; finally, we can consider motivation, whether the author or speaker has anything to gain from lying, from honesty, or from making the claims they do. These considerations do not transfer smoothly to the assessment of *Wikipedia* articles.

We can get some idea of reputation, credentials, and track record for *Wikipedia* in patches. In 2005, the esteemed science journal *Nature* published a comparative study of *Wikipedia* and *Encyclopedia Britannica* (slogan: 'Know for Sure') on a wide range of scientific topics. Both sources contained errors, *Wikipedia* more than *Britannica*, but the difference was not overwhelming. More generally, each of us has expertise in some area, whether professional or personal – the sports team you follow, the town you grew up in, the genre of music you were immersed in as a teenager. In these areas, we can check the accuracy of *Wikipedia* articles against our own knowledge. But such checks don't easily generalize. The accuracy of one article gives us little reason to expect accuracy of another, which will have been created by different people, paying different levels of attention, and with different levels of controversy.

Inherent plausibility and coherence with what we already believe can give us some clues, so long as what we already believe is reasonably well founded. Again, however, the fact that one element or article is a good fit with things we already believe does not lend credibility to other elements or other articles, since there is no particular reason to think that the processes that have made one article accurate are likely to have been replicated across the board.

Issues about expertise are hard to assess. We know that there are no entry barriers to editing *Wikipedia*, but we also know that errors can be corrected by anyone who spots them. In such a system, will the views of those who are in a position to know come to dominate the views of those who are not in a position to know? This will differ widely across different topics. For example, it's unlikely that false beliefs about asteroid spectral types are widespread. Most of us don't know anything about the topic, but we're not under any illusions that we do know. The paraphernalia that surrounds each *Wikipedia* article can provide some clues about this, if we bother to consult it. Each article has an associated discussion page, where changes are debated, and a record of earlier versions of the same article.

Perhaps the single biggest challenge in assessing *Wikipedia* entries comes when we consider motivation and honesty. When assessing the likely accuracy of more traditional sources – offline or online – we can consider the possible motivations of the author, or the institution that lies behind the source. If I know that literature has been published by a campaign group or a company with commercial interests in the matter, I can take this into account. If I know that the author, or editor, or publisher, has something to gain from maintaining a reputation for accuracy and honesty, or something to lose from being found out in a lie or an error, then I can take that into account too.

These clues are not easily available on *Wikipedia*. We may be able to judge that some topics are so uncontroversial that editors' motives are likely to be disinterested. But even that can be a tough call – for all I know, astrophysicists' marriages have ended in divorce over the nature of asteroid spectral types. And lack of controversy doesn't provide anyone with a motive for accuracy, as opposed to careless error. Where topics are controversial, or someone has an interest at stake, we can rarely know what motivates those who have made the edits; one exception occurred in 2006, when *Wikipedia* traced changes in biographies of US senators to computers based within the Senate.

Some of these concerns are addressed by WikiProjects: teams of editors who collectively adopt the articles on a particular science, geographical region, period of history, or science-fiction series, for example. Teams work together to review articles, make corrections where they think it necessary, add detail, and create new articles, though non-members are also still free to edit as they see fit.

Teams give quality ratings for articles in 'their' area. You can tell whether an article is under the auspices of a WikiProject by checking its discussion page. I personally find this somewhat comforting – perhaps this reveals my taste for hierarchies and order – but, of course, WikiProject membership is up for grabs, and some teams are much more active than others.

A newer development has not yet borne fruit. In 2010, *Wikipedia* introduced a 'rate this page' feature, and rolled this out to 100,000 pages in July 2011. Readers can rate each page to the degree it is trustworthy, objective, complete, and well written (there is also an option to check 'I am highly knowledgeable about this topic' – honestly and accurately, of course), and see the average rating given by other readers. In time, this may help casual readers gauge the trustworthiness of individual articles. In the meantime, however, the best advice is: handle with care.

Online dating

Lonely hearts have been advertising for soulmates for more than three hundred years; there has always been an element of risk involved, and a corresponding need for both trust and caution on both sides. But the advent of online dating has magnified some of the same old issues, whilst introducing new ones. Before they even get started, potential daters must trust the site itself, and the agency that runs it. Different agencies make different promises, about the quality, quantity, and variety of potential dates available, and about the likely success of their proactive matchmaking efforts. Eharmony ('#1 Trusted Online Dating Site for Singles') suggests dates based on personality questionnaires, whilst some other sites simply allow members to browse at will, hoping to spot potential matches themselves. Different sites operate on different financial models – some are free to users and funded by adverts, whilst others charge a membership fee, or a fee per contact – these different arrangements create different incentives both for the site and the user. Even 'free' sites require significant commitments of time and emotional energy from the user, who must trust that this will eventually pay dividends.

Then there are online dating scams, sophisticated variants of the '419' scams we all know and hate from our email accounts. You get to know someone online, who eventually asks you to pay for their plane ticket to the UK, or to help out with their mother's medical bills. The scammer has the opportunity to build up a relationship with you over several months before asking for money, rather than cold-calling your email inbox, and can play on your desire to believe that he or she has a romantic interest in you. Even if no money changes hands, such scams are emotionally damaging in ways which can affect our long-term ability to trust; they are much more harmful than the mere nuisances that clog up inboxes.

There are more mundane deceptions or omissions. One study of online daters in New York checked their actual height, weight, and age against the details each had given in their online profiles. Nearly half had lied about their height (by half an inch or more), and 60% had lied about their weight (by 5 pounds or more); men were more likely to exaggerate their height, and women to downplay their weight. Relatively few (18%) had lied about their age: researchers guessed that this might be because they had mostly interviewed young-ish subjects. Overall, four out of every five subjects had lied about one of these three characteristics, though the lie was usually a fairly small deviation from the truth.

To see whether people were simply fooling themselves, the researchers checked what people thought their own height and weight were: it turned out that most people knew the truth, but were concealing that in their online profiles. In less measurable dimensions, however, we may be practising self-deception: who amongst us even knows how to write a truthful description of their own personality, and who really knows exactly what they're looking for in a partner?

When we trust someone's self-description on a dating site, we're trusting both in their honesty and in their self-knowledge. These situations underline the fact that trust is rarely all-or-nothing; we make judgements of plausibility, growing in trust or distrust as we have more interaction and gather more information. And we can use what we know about people's likely motives: we know that they know that outrageous lies about physical appearance will be discovered if we ever meet face to face, but lies about marital status or honourable intentions will take longer to uncover.

Finally, online dating presents challenges of trustworthiness as well as challenges of trusting. Of course, *you* are trustworthy, but how can you communicate that to potential dates? Online communication limits the kinds of evidence that are available about you, allowing for few independent checks; when we meet in person, we can assess clothes, manner, accent, and so on, along with what's actually said and done. Little of this is available online. And, in these new situations, it can be hard to judge what trustworthiness requires of us: must we respond to every enquiry? How truthful should our profiles be?

Online or offline, there is a danger of a lonely hearts arms race. At the very least, it's reasonable to expect that others are putting a positive spin on their own situation, appearance, and personality; I'm unlikely to mention my irritating habits, my neuroses, or my aggressive dog upfront, and if I did, this self-undermining behaviour might be more off-putting than the habits, the neuroses, or the dog. Once a (heterosexual) woman knows that half of all men are exaggerating their height, she's likely to subtract a little from whatever the next man claims. And if he knows that's likely, then he may well exaggerate a little more, just to compensate. This is a case where mutual knowledge may decrease both trust and trustworthiness.

Customer reviews

From Amazon to Argos, many retail sites carry customer reviews (and you can even check out online reviews of the various online dating sites). Handled well, the very existence of such reviews, positive and negative, can increase the apparent trustworthiness of the site, as well as providing genuinely useful feedback to both retailer and customers. Marks and Spencer has a delightful community of maturing women (reviewers declare age and gender in a side-bar) who provide helpful advice to other shoppers about sizing, fabric softness, how well garments survive the wash, and what colour they appear in daylight. (This isn't just in the women and kids departments: women review plenty of men's clothing, often referring to a husband or son.) This makes it easier for other customers – OK, for me – to make an informed, confident choice; occasionally M&S will respond to negative comments with apologies, explanations, or announcements that the garment is now discontinued or manufactured differently. All of this increases the apparent trustworthiness of the brand.

Marks and Spencer retails its own-brand gear, but both Amazon and Argos are clearing-houses for thousands of different brands, many of which are in direct competition with one another. A Nikon camera or a Canon? Hotpoint or Whirlpool for your new tumble-dryer? Customer reviews play their part in our decision-making, but there is no special difference between reviews on the retailer's site, and non-expert reviews found elsewhere on the web (as opposed to the reviews on specialist hi-fi, motoring, or gadget sites, which are more like those found in offline magazines).

What can we learn from reading customer reviews? Tastes and standards differ, but a preponderance of either positive or negative reviews is hard to ignore: if most people like their Hotpoint tumble-dryer, and if I don't have idiosyncratic tastes or needs (in my tumble-drying at least), then the odds are I'll like it too. Customer reviews promise a more disinterested opinion on the goods than the blurb we get from either manufacturer or retailer.

That is, if the reviews are genuine. Reviews are usually posted pseudonymously, giving us few clues about the expertise or motivation of the reviewer. Amazon has a number of mechanisms designed to increase the usefulness of reviews – readers can vote on the helpfulness of a given review, and click through to other reviews by the same reviewer. Reviewers are ranked for their perceived helpfulness, and 'the most trusted' are invited to join the Amazon Vine programme, receiving free products in return for writing 'honest and unbiased' reviews of them. There are quirks in this system: obviously fake but entertaining reviews are often rated helpful. But it effectively reduces the risk involved in trusting reviews, by spreading the decision amongst many reviewer-raters. (There's also potential for regress here: who rates the reviewer-raters?)

Vetted contributors post only a small proportion of the reviews, however, and many of us will look only at the aggregated star ratings, which weigh all voices equally. We are not in a position to judge whether any given reviewer has a financial or other motive to praise or condemn a particular product. In 2010, academic Orlando Figes was caught out pseudonymously applauding his own books on Russian history, and criticizing those of his rivals, on Amazon UK; the affair became a minor scandal, not least because of Figes's initial denials, his involvement of lawyers, and his short-lived attempt to blame his own wife. Setting aside his dubious over-reactions, what exactly had Figes done wrong in posting his anonymous reviews? Criticizing other people's books can generate gossip and resentment, but it is a normal part of intellectual life, and doesn't usually attract opprobrium at the level Figes received. Moreover, Figes clearly has more expertise than most of us in Russian history. The problem was neither the critical tone, nor a lack of expertise, but a perception of dishonesty.

Dishonesty? Presumably Figes honestly thinks that his own book is 'beautifully written...a gift to us all', and that his rival's is 'awful'. And he did not pretend to be someone he is not – he did not dishonestly pose as one of his colleagues, or claim to be Mikhail Gorbachev. Even his pseudonym – 'historian' – accurately, if incompletely, describes him. Instead, Figes failed to reveal his own identity, though that identity would have played a significant role in readers' assessment of his review. Most Amazon reviewers fail to reveal their own identities, but only in some cases would knowledge of identity make any difference to the reader's decision whether to trust the reviewer. Figes violated a norm according to which reviewers should declare their interests and allow the audience to decide how to weigh this.

The Figes affair was a storm in a samovar, but fake reviews can cause lasting damage to small businesses, as well as misleading the readers who trust them. TripAdvisor invites reviews of hotels, restaurants, and the like from people who have visited them recently. Individual reviews are published below an aggregated star rating; the TripAdvisor page is typically near the top of the Google results for that establishment. Holidays are a significant expense, we're often travelling somewhere new, and scanning the reviews can help us choose. TripAdvisor claims to offer 'reviews you can trust' to help you find 'hotels travellers trust': how reliable can it be?

One obvious concern is that, like Figes, hoteliers can anonymously praise their own accommodation, and criticize their business rivals. TripAdvisor's guidelines forbid this, but it cannot easily be monitored. (The guidelines also forbid 'graphic reports of violent criminal activity', and note that 'reports of deaths will be considered on an individual basis', but reviews can be damaging without plumbing quite those depths.) In 2011, KwikChex, a 'brand reputation management company', lodged a formal complaint with the Advertising Standards Authority, on behalf of a group of business owners who had suffered what they believed to be fake negative reviews. These are not just complaints about the décor or cleanliness, but include accusations of racism – and racist accusations – along with theft, food-poisoning, and fraud.

Fake reviews are more damaging for business owners than they are for the consumers who take them at face value. A consumer is more likely to miss out on a good hotel because of fake reviews than to mistakenly book into a bad hotel. This is because it's hard to ignore negative reviews, even if they're in the minority (as a university lecturer, I've had the same experience reading student reviews of my teaching): forty positive comments can't quite erase one wholehearted criticism, because we'd all like our holidays (and our lectures) to be perfect. Missing out on one good hotel amongst many is a shame, but preferable to booking into a bad hotel, not least because you're unlikely to discover that you missed a good hotel. Moreover, a single bad review can damage the same hotel over and over again, as it is read by different potential guests; an individual browser would have to be very unlucky to read malicious false reviews for a whole range of hotels.

Consumers are damaged in more indirect ways by false reviews, however, as these diminish the credibility of the entire site, including the very many honest reviews written by genuine guests. Whether it's linen-blend wide-leg belted trousers at Marks and Spencer, tumble-dryers at Argos, books on Russian history at Amazon, or boutique hotels on TripAdvisor, we all stand to gain from reading informed, honest reviews, so long as we can tell the difference between these and the fakes. Quantity can be some guarantee of quality, so long as honest reviewers continue to post, and fraudsters do not have the resources to generate equivalent numbers of fake reviews. But this balance may be tipped if genuine reviewers do not feel trusted – why bother to post reviews if they are likely to be regarded with suspicion?

Chapter 8
Institutions, conspiracies, and nations

Rich interpersonal trust lies at the heart of our lives, underpinning our relationships with friends and family; likewise, the value of trustworthiness guides us in forming and maintaining those relationships. Looser ties of trust, reliance, and cooperation are also crucial to our daily interaction with acquaintances and strangers. But what about our attitudes of trust – or distrust – as directed towards institutions, public figures, and entire social groups? Is there a difference between trusting the political system and trusting politicians, or between trusting the Church and trusting clergymen? Can institutions themselves display trustworthiness, or only the individuals who populate those institutions?

Trust in professionals

When surveyed, we say we trust doctors more than scientists, newsreaders more than journalists, and 'politicians generally' least of all. (Pollsters themselves get a middling trust rating, or so they tell us.) The standard survey question targets our trust that doctors, scientists, and so on will tell the truth: this measures perceived honesty, rather than perceived competence.

Honesty is a personal character trait with significant moral weight. Why are we prepared to make sweeping moral judgements about social groups in this way, rather than judging individuals case by case? Do we think that people's characters are determined by their professions, or that choice of profession is determined by their character? A bit of both, perhaps. But it's also likely that we're thinking about people's honesty when they're speaking specifically in their professional capacity. After all, there are doctors (trusted by 88% of us) and teachers (trusted by 81% of us) who become politicians (trusted by 14% of us); newsreaders (62%) are often journalists (19%); and both judges (72%) and government ministers (17%) sometimes walk amongst ordinary men or women in the street (55%). Trust me, I'm a professor (74%).

Very many of us are suspicious of politicians. But if my local doctor is also a politician, this doesn't make me doubt the sincerity of the medical advice she gives me. Moreover, although we report high levels of confidence in doctors' honesty, we presumably don't think that doctors are unusually truthful with their spouses about extramarital affairs, especially likely to give brutally honest reviews of their children's school plays, or quicker than the rest of us to own up and pay for breakages in a holiday rental. Trusting doctors 'in general' means trusting them to be honest when they speak in their professional capacity.

The boundaries of 'professional capacity' can be blurry. When my doctor tells me about my state of health, she is clearly speaking in her professional capacity, and I'm likely to trust her. But what should we make of doctors who speak in public about the wisdom – or foolishness – of proposed structural changes to state healthcare, participating in political debate? On the one hand, doctors carry an aura of trustworthiness which most politicians lack, and they have detailed first-hand experience of how healthcare currently operates. On the other hand, doctors as a profession may have an interest in retaining the status quo, or reason to avoid particular 'reforms'. The British Medical Association opposed the founding of the UK National Health Service in 1948; health minister Nye Bevan later said that he bought the doctors' cooperation by 'stuffing their mouths with gold', allowing them to retain their private practices whilst working for the NHS.

People who share a profession work within similar institutional structures, often with similar motives and incentives, subject to similar risks, opportunities, and expectations, in their professional lives at least. If we trust doctors to be honest, this is in part because we believe they have little to gain and much to lose from lying to their patients or colleagues; in their personal lives, however, they are in much the same situation as the rest of us, which means we have little reason to think that they will be unusually honest (or dishonest) in that realm. Our difficulty in understanding what motives and incentives doctors have when intervening in political debate is reflected in our difficulty in knowing how to weigh their opinions against those of politicians.

Structures and motives aren't the whole story. Personal experience also influences our judgement about professional honesty: most of us will have had some positive experiences with doctors, and most of us can think of plenty of examples where politicians have been caught in outright lies or deception, including deceptions in their private lives. But our thinking is not altogether clear: our views about those shady government ministers (trusted by only 17% of us) are driven almost entirely by what those duplicitous journalists (19%) write and broadcast, and, indeed, by what politicians (14%) say about one another. If we were genuinely and thoroughly sceptical about journalists, we would be at a loss to know what to believe about even the most basic aspects of public life, foreign affairs, or life outside our immediate neighbourhood. And without journalists, we would have very little idea what scientists say or believe, which would make it puzzling that we give them a 71% rating for honesty. Our supposed lack of trust in journalists can at most be an attitude of caution, peppered with deep dismay at the behaviour of the phone-hacking, paparazzi contingent; after all, the downfall of the *News of the World* in summer 2011 was precipitated by journalist Nick Davies and others at the *Guardian*. Perceived motivations and incentives are important here too: what if any penalties are likely for 'bad behaviour', and what rewards are available for ill-gotten stories?

It is striking that expertise-based professions – doctor, teacher, professor, judge, scientist – are clustered at the high-trust end of the polls, whilst the foot of the table is dominated by professions such as trade union official, business leader, journalist, and politician, where success is perceived to require skill and energy, but not years of study or accumulation of factual knowledge. We trust the honesty of those professionals whose competence and expertise we cannot directly judge: I must take my doctor's word for it about what's wrong with my knee, but I feel free to disagree vehemently with my MP's view about grammar schools.

Again, this suggests that our confidence in the honesty of certain professionals is based on our confidence in the institutional structures, motives, and risks which surround them: our confidence cannot be based on independent checks of the truthfulness of what doctors and other experts tell us, because we usually have no way of making such independent checks. We trust in both the honesty and the competence of certain professionals – in their professional lives – because of the system of credentials, qualifications, and monitoring in which they are embedded. It's hard to have similar general confidence in less ordered professions, and in those cases we must make case-by-case judgements about individual people.

Trust in institutions

The trust we report in certain professions amounts to trust in the individual members of those professions, as they carry out their professional duties. But some institutions seem greater than the sum of their parts, to have a life of their own beyond those of their members, and so we may wonder about our trust in the institutions themselves. Can we trust the BBC? The NHS? NASA? What about looser groupings or organizations: big business, the banks, the legal system, the media, 'politics'? We can ask the same question about individual companies, governments, or nations.

Different organizations and institutions differ greatly in their degrees of coherence and common purpose. One basic question about any such entity is how far its behaviour can be predicted, for better or for worse. But predictability is not always a good thing – individuals or institutions can be predictably ill-behaved, and unpredictability can be inherently valuable in an arts organization, a think-tank, or an advertising agency, where a surprise can shake us out of our tired routines. Sometimes we rely on organizations to be unpredictable. But in any case, trust must go beyond mere prediction.

Rich, interpersonal trust is bound up with commitment. Trusting people involves relying upon them to meet their commitments, to follow through on their undertakings. Trustworthiness involves matching our actions to our commitments, not least by exercising caution in incurring new commitments. It is commitment which enables us to distinguish this relationship of trust from the more mundane relationship of reliance: I rely on my alarm clock to wake me up, and my key to open the door, but I don't think of this in terms of commitment, obligations, or promises, and so I don't think of this as trust, merely as reliance. Rich, interpersonal trust has moral overtones: it's a good thing to be trustworthy, to keep your promises, and we're entitled to resent people who prove untrustworthy, who do not live up to their commitments.

Can institutions or organizations make commitments, promises, undertakings? Yes, in many cases: companies enter into legal contracts, which are not personal agreements between the individuals who happen to be in charge at the time of signing. Nations sign treaties with other nations, and these agreements outlast the individual leaders who have negotiated and signed.

More widely, many organizations have charters, statements of purpose, or constitutions which set out goals and guidelines.

For example, the BBC has a charter (as well as an agreement, protocols, policies, codes, and guidance) that sets out its public purposes, its governance structure, and its powers. Purposes include sustaining citizenship, promoting education, stimulating creativity, and 'bringing the UK to the world and the world to the UK'. It seems appropriate to think in terms of trust and distrust in judging whether the BBC is doing a decent job in fulfilling those purposes: the better it is doing on these counts, the more trustworthy it is in these respects. Failure in these respects would demonstrate a degree of untrustworthiness, not merely the unreliability of a dodgy alarm clock or worn-out key.

This kind of trust – and trustworthiness – involves both honesty and competence. When we trust institutions to live up to their commitments, to carry out their duties, we trust both that they will make good-faith efforts to do so, and that they have the ability to succeed. As with individual people, neither honesty nor competence alone is enough for full trustworthiness: well-meaning but dysfunctional organizations cannot be trusted, and nor can highly effective groups that disguise their true goals and actions. And as with individual people, it seems reasonable for us to resent institutions and organizations that betray our trust, and to appreciate those that live up to their commitments.

Can an institution, company, or organization really be well-meaning, or malicious, if this is supposed to be more than the sum of the attitudes of its individual members or employees? The notion of institutional racism reflects the idea that organizations can embody values and attitudes that are not explicitly endorsed by many or most of the people involved in the organization; likewise, an organization can have procedures, policies, and structures which give proper regard to its commitments, or which fail to align with its stated goals and purposes. Such procedures and policies can outlast any particular group of employees or members, and affect the behaviour and attitudes of incoming people.

Trusting 'the system'

Some institutions, companies, and organizations have enough structure and common purpose that we can readily think of them as quasi-personal, with commitments, intentions, and capabilities, earning our trust or our distrust as the case may be. But we may also talk of trusting or distrusting much more amorphous entities – politics (rather than particular politicians, or particular parties), big business (rather than individual business leaders, or particular companies), the legal system, or the media. Does it make sense to place either trust or distrust in such systems, or should we think of this in terms of mere reliability and unreliability, as we do with a machine or a natural phenomenon?

This question has no straightforward answer, but we can distinguish several issues. Are the systems in question performing the function they are intended to perform, fulfilling their main purpose? For example, arguably the overall purpose of the legal system is to ensure fair treatment for all before the law. We should trust the legal system if we think that, on the whole, this purpose is achieved; we should be distrustful if we think it is not. Arguably, the overall purpose of the media is to ensure free flow of information and opinions; it's reasonable to trust the media as a whole to the extent we think that this purpose is being fulfilled. (We can go on to ask more detailed questions about whether we trust individual journalists, or individual newspapers/TV channels, and we can give different answers in different cases.)

Perhaps this sounds too idealistic. You may suspect that the real purpose of the legal system is to ensure that power remains in the hands of a wealthy elite without the need for violent oppression of the working classes. You may suspect that the real purpose of the media is to make money for media proprietors, and to enable them to exercise disproportionate influence on elected politicians. And you may believe that, relative to these goals, both the legal system and the media are enormously successful. Does this mean that you trust these systems? No. If you are right, and this is the real purpose of the legal system or media, then you are entitled to feel distrustful because of the mismatch between the real purposes of these systems and the noble ideals embodied in their public self-representations. No newspaper explicitly presents itself as concerned primarily to make money and exert undue influence on politicians; carved over the door of the Old Bailey courthouse is the motto 'defend the children of the poor and punish the wrongdoer', not 'protect the rich and crush the poor'.

This contrasts with overtly criminal organizations, like the Mafia, which make little pretence of benefiting non-members. While it is right for us to resent the appalling acts and influence of such organizations, it would be peculiar to feel let down or betrayed by them. What else did we expect? In contrast, we have been betrayed by the legal system if indeed it serves primarily to protect the rich and crush the poor.

We have moved quite far from the prototypical trust relation which holds between two individuals who know each other well; we are trying to extend concepts and ideas developed in that context, not just to structured organizations but to entire social systems, so it is hardly surprising if we're feeling the stretch. In more individual cases, we have been able to convert questions about trust into questions about trustworthiness – what is it for a person, or an institution, to be trustworthy? – and have seen that commitment-meeting is a central element of trustworthiness. The more diffuse and decentralized a system is, however, the more difficult it is to understand it as incurring and fulfilling commitments, and so the more difficult it is to apply the language of trustworthiness or untrustworthiness.

A final complication is that systems like 'the media' or 'politics' are of course populated by individual journalists, proprietors, politicians, lobbyists, and so on, who do make assertions, honest or dishonest, and incur commitments, to be fulfilled or not. It is very rare that we entirely trust – or distrust – an individual, in every respect, regarding both honesty and competence, and to the same full degree. Rather, our attitudes of trust and distrust are modulated (remember our trust in doctors, which may vary across different parts of personal and professional life). We need to develop the same subtlety and modulation in our attitudes to institutions.

Conspiracy theories

Conspiracies – and conspiracy theories – raise some special issues about both trust in individuals and trust in institutions or groups. Conspirators require a degree of trust in one another, but such trust may be difficult to achieve where the stakes are high, because of the risks associated with discovery. And belief in conspiracy theories requires fundamental distrust about conventional pictures of the world, along with a contrastingly high level of confidence in the ability of governments or secret groups to control the public flow of information.

What is a conspiracy? A conspiracy is a secret plan or action, involving more than one person, to achieve some negative goal. After all, 'conspiracy' is a derogatory term, and presumably people involved in such groups who believe in the value of their goals do not think of themselves as conspiring. (It's an irregular verb: we are involved in underground activism, you are plotting, they are conspiring.) Within any such group, there is a need for the members to trust each other's mutual honesty, and trust each other's competence in the roles they play within the group. But members must also trust each other to be dishonest, or secretive, with respect to the outside world. Again, we see that trust and trustworthiness are not all-or-nothing; people can be trustworthy in one respect without being trustworthy in all respects to all comers, and indeed trustworthiness in one respect (keeping a secret) can positively require untrustworthiness in another respect (lying to the outside world).

What, then, is a conspiracy theory? We might adopt a relatively wide-ranging definition, according to which a conspiracy theory is any suggestion that there is a conspiracy. On this definition, some conspiracy theories are true, and are perfectly reasonable to believe; Watergate and the Iran-Contra affair are often cited in this context, whilst any accurate account of a surprise coup or assassination (except for the 'lone gunman') will also qualify.

A more focused definition requires that a conspiracy has, broadly speaking, succeeded on a large scale: it has achieved its goals, and managed to do so without revealing its true role in bringing about those goals. The assassination of JFK is perhaps the most conspiracy-theorized event of modern times. One theory has it that the Mafia were behind the killing, in league with the CIA, the FBI, Cuba, and/or LBJ (take your pick). Part of what makes this a conspiracy theory is the view that forces behind the assassination have succeeded in preventing their role coming to light (although a Fox News poll in 2004 found that only 14% of Americans think we know all the facts about the assassination, and only 25% think it was the act of a single individual).

We could adopt an even narrower definition, so that a conspiracy theory is by definition irrational, or crazy – this may fit the popular image of conspiracy theories, and helps explain why people are often reluctant to self-identify as conspiracy theorists. But building the craziness of conspiracy theories into the very definition makes it tough to ask the interesting questions about what we should believe, who it is reasonable to trust, and which conspiracy theories might be true. It also blurs the distinction between sheer speculation – Elvis lives! – and theories which don't seem so crazy once you start looking into them. (You can insert your own example here.) So let's work with the less judgemental definition, that a conspiracy theory involves the view that there has been a successful conspiracy, one that has achieved its main goal, and also managed to keep its true nature disguised.

As with any complex idea, deciding whether to believe in a conspiracy theory requires us to balance up evidence pointing in different directions, and weigh up the relative reliability of different sources of information. Who and what can we trust? There is no universal, mechanical strategy for doing this, which is why reasonable people can sometimes disagree about what to believe, in the courtroom, or in science, politics, religion, or more mundane matters. Making your mind up involves recognizing the evidence which supports the view you favour. But it also involves explaining away the evidence and sources that point in the opposite direction: if the accused is innocent, why were his fingerprints found at the scene?; if Sally is vegetarian, why did we run into her at the steak house? We cannot always explain every aspect of countervailing evidence, but when we are trying to be reasonable, we have a duty to try.

Conspiracy theories make it seem very easy to fulfil this duty. Such theories often have a self-insulating character, because they provide a ready-made explanation for apparently problematic evidence. *Of course* it looks as if there was no conspiracy: that's because it was such a good conspiracy. *Of course* the Warren Commission found that Lee Harvey Oswald was a lone killer: the Mafia/FBI/CIA effectively covered their tracks and/or influenced the Commission (which included a former director of the CIA). *Of course* the Apollo 11 astronauts continue to claim that they really landed on the Moon: to admit otherwise would be to lose their heroic status, and risk who-knows-what retribution.

As philosopher Brian Keeley points out, the conspiracy theorist sees him- (or occasionally her-) self as investigating a domain that is actively trying to frustrate the investigation, and this can seem to justify a sceptical approach to apparent evidence. From this point of view, we should approach data, and sources, with a distrustful eye. And once we begin with that attitude, it is difficult to find evidence that will shift us towards a more trusting outlook. More generally, if we take a default attitude of mistrust to what other people tell us, we are unlikely to be able to gather independent evidence of their reliability.

This distrust focuses on dishonesty, via the idea of cover-up, rather than incompetence. Indeed, conspiracy theories require a significant degree of respect for the power of those supposedly involved in the conspiracy. It's no surprise that the organizations implicated in JFK conspiracy theories are those we already know to be powerful and effective. It wouldn't be plausible to accuse the local domino club of orchestrating the JFK cover-up, unless we also posited a complex relationship between the domino club and larger, more powerful bodies. A lone gunman, or a small group of conspirators, can carry out an assassination, but widescale concealment requires power.

The power, and competency, of the groups involved is a part of the story about how the assassination/Moon-landing fake/ Elvis-abduction was achieved, but perhaps more significantly, it is a necessary part of the story about how the cover-up is achieved and perpetuated. Indeed, in many cases, the cover-up looks like the more challenging task, and, therefore, the weak point in the conspiracy theory: thinking about the sheer number of people who would have had to get involved in faking the Moon-landings, how plausible is it that all of those people could be induced to silence?

Any estimation of whether to trust someone involves a judgement about their likely motives, their character, and the external incentives they face. Conspiracy theories typically include a story about the evil or self-serving motives of those involved. But even granting this, the cost and risks of the cover-up must be weighed in the balance – if these organizations are powerful and ruthless, why do they bother achieving their aims by secret means? Conspiracy theorizing requires an overall stance of distrustfulness, one that is hard to shake with reasoning alone.

Trust in international relations

Studies in international relations are often centrally concerned with how conflicts begin and end, treaty negotiations, how international organizations function, and how states interact in various contexts. Trust – and distrust – sometimes play a significant role in explaining these phenomena, either as part of a general model of interaction, or as applied to specific case studies. Why did the Cold War develop, and how was it eventually resolved without turning into a hot war? Why did the Western European states manage to move relatively quickly from all-out war in the 1940s, to ever-increasing degrees of economic and political cooperation? How do inter-ethnic rivalries grow, and can they be contained?

We can think of trusting – or distrusting – relationships as holding between states, between individual leaders or negotiators, or between 'non-state actors', including NGOs, multinational corporations, terrorist groups, and religious or ethnic groupings which may transcend state boundaries. And trust or distrust may hold between members of different categories. For example, an individual diplomat or president may distrust an entire ethnic group, or trust a foreign state, whilst an NGO such as the International Red Cross/Red Crescent is trusted both by states and by individuals. Perhaps because of this very wide range of possible (dis)trusters and (dis)trustees, there is significant disagreement about what is the most fruitful way of thinking about trust in international relations: many of the different approaches we have seen in other areas and disciplines have been applied to this domain.

One approach works primarily with ideas about calculated risk, and prediction of what other states, non-state actors, or individuals will do. On this picture, to trust is to make a judgement about what another is likely to do, based on their perceived incentives and interests, and to decide that taking a certain risk, involving a degree of vulnerability, is worthwhile. This is the kind of trust that is at stake in the economists' 'trust games', where participants are given an initial amount of money, which they can either keep, or gamble on 'investing' with a partner, in the hope of reaping increased returns.

A different approach is more emotional, or moralized, focusing on trust as relative optimism that another will do the right thing, or act benevolently. This may be the kind of trust envisaged by British politicians and diplomats who speak hopefully about the 'special relationship' between the UK and the US: this is supposed to be a relationship built on a long-lasting friendship between the two nations, involving cultural affinities and shared values, not just a marriage of convenience between states which happen to find their current interests aligned on the international stage. Indeed, part what is hoped for from the special relationship is that the US will help the UK even when this isn't obviously in the American national interest (though it's easier to think of examples when this has worked in the opposite direction).

These different ideas about trust will deliver different verdicts about situations in which states are able to cooperate, and predict one another's behaviour, simply because there is mutual knowledge of the constraints each is working under. During the Cold War, the US and USSR had good reason to think that each had second-strike capability. That is, each would be able to respond to a nuclear attack by launching a devastating nuclear attack of its own: it would not be possible for the aggressor to completely destroy the target's nuclear capacity in one fell swoop. The doctrine of Mutually Assured Destruction (MAD) placed public constraints on the behaviour of both states, given the fairly safe assumption that both wanted to survive and prosper, and this meant that the behaviour of each became predictable in various respects. (Compare this situation to one in which there is a single overwhelming power, or a state so crazed or dysfunctional that it cannot be assumed to prioritize its own survival.)

Is this a situation of trust? If we think primarily in terms of calculated risk and prediction, then yes. The super-powers were able to get a good sense of their mutual vulnerabilities, strengths, and interests, and to make informed decisions on this basis. But if we think primarily in terms of relationships, benevolence, emotion, and morality, then no. Each super-power had very different values and ideology, and realized that there was no love lost between them. Neither thought that the other was restraining itself out of human kindness, goodwill, or the desire to do the right thing.

For the most part, we can recognize that different concepts of trust are useful in various contexts: we can see that one sort of trust was readily available during the Cold War, and that another sort was much harder to come by. There is no special reason to insist that only one of these is Real Trust, since both concepts can do important work. However, the important thing is to recognize that there is more than one concept here, and to be especially careful in taking our intuitions or studies of one kind of trust and mistakenly assuming they will apply to the other.

For example, social psychologists have studied the differences in people's willingness to trust and cooperate with one another, noticing that this can vary between different people, and between different circumstances. Can we apply these findings to international relations? Surely there is much to be gained by investigating this, but we need to take care that the 'trust' that is studied by one academic discipline is the 'trust' that is of interest to another. We must also be cautious in scaling up the attitudes of trust and cooperation at work between individual people to apply to relations between people and states, or between states themselves. States, like corporations, are often treated as quasi-persons, but there are limits to this analogy.

Finally, trust in international relations can concern honesty, competence, or both. Whether a state can be trusted to comply with its treaty obligations depends upon whether it has, or ever had, the intention of complying. But it also depends upon whether it has the material and other resources to enable it to comply. Weak leaders cannot be trusted if they do not have the political capital they need to deliver on their promises, and failed states cannot enter into agreements at all, meaning that they are candidates for neither trust nor distrust.

Conclusion
The importance of being trustworthy

In the end, what matters most: trust or trustworthiness?
Trusting is the right thing to do when it aligns with or generates
trustworthiness, while trusting the untrustworthy is a recipe for
betrayal, disappointment, and exploitation. Trust can also misfire
when we misunderstand the interests and commitments of others,
even though they are not inherently untrustworthy. If I do not
know or care about your wishes, if I have tried to make clear that
I cannot or will not help you, then it would be a mistake for you to
trust me, but I would not have proven myself to be untrustworthy.
Unhelpful and unfriendly, perhaps, but not deceptive, not
incompetent, not untrustworthy. In such a situation, you should
neither trust nor distrust me: you can predict that I will not help
you, but you needn't regard this as a violation of trust.

Is trustworthiness valuable in its own right, or only where it
attracts the trust of others? We have encountered various different
kinds of trustworthiness in this book, only some of which have
value in their own right. For example, in the 'trust games' studied
by economists, trustworthiness amounts to a willingness to return
a portion of someone's unsolicited gift. (Remember that the first
player can choose to hand over some cash, which is then tripled by
the experimenter; the second player chooses how much, if any, to
return to the first player.) There is no external obligation upon the
second player to return some cash – the first player is not starving

or homeless – and there is no pre-existing agreement between the two players. Moreover, the second player's decision does not affect the total amount of money made available by the experimenter. So trustworthiness in this context is valuable only in so far as it facilitates future rounds of the game, encouraging the first player to take further chances, and enabling the experimenter to inject more cash. Depending on the structure of the game, this may or may not benefit the second player in the long run.

That future cooperation, and added cash, may be of significant value themselves, at least in the real-life situations that the games are intended to model. If there is an important goal that can be furthered by cooperation of this sort, then that goal provides a rationale for developing this kind of trustworthiness. But it all turns on the nature of the goal: if cooperation is being developed between two businesses as a way of fleecing their customers, or between a terrorist organization and a rogue state as a way of furthering their mutual interest in violent ends, then cooperation is something we would want to disrupt, not encourage.

Other, richer forms of trustworthiness seem to be valuable in their own right. Honesty, for example, is not just useful in so far as it promotes other goals: it is something worth having in its own right. That's not to say that honesty is always the most important consideration, that it is never worth sacrificing for other goals. After all, when the murderer is at the door, asking for your friend, you can and should lie about his whereabouts. But giving up honesty because other goals require this is always something of a sacrifice, a matter for some regret. Or so it should be.

More generally, the practice of living up to our commitments – being thoughtful about what we take on, but then making sure we follow through – is a form of trustworthiness that has inherent value. The same goes for living up to our commitments in what we say, being thoughtful about what we choose to talk about, being honest, and not representing ourselves as more knowledgeable than we really are. But this kind of trustworthiness can also be of immense practical value, especially where the commitments are worthwhile, to you or to others.

Such trustworthiness has practical value where it attracts trust; being trusted is a precondition for all sorts of rewarding pursuits, and it is difficult to get much done in situations where others do not trust what you say, or do not trust you to follow through on your commitments. Being trustworthy makes you deserving of others' trust, and where you can effectively signal this, then trust will follow.

We cannot signal our trustworthiness case by case, or not in the cases that matter most. Trust can be most valuable, and most risky, in situations in which the trustee is unable to directly demonstrate trustworthiness. I can directly demonstrate my honesty to you only in situations in which you have an independent source to corroborate my testimony; but if you have an independent source, then it's not so important whether or not you trust me. I can demonstrate my skill and knowledge if you let me, but in many situations, you won't be able to give me this opportunity without extending some initial trust.

This is why consistency is important. We judge one another's trustworthiness partly on track record. But this kind of inductive reasoning, from past to present to future, is plausible only when there is a genuine pattern to track. If I were random about meeting my commitments – sometimes making great efforts to keep my promises, sometimes brushing them off – or an occasional but random liar, you could not build up your confidence and trust in me even after seeing a number of cases in which I behave in a trustworthy fashion.

According to social psychologists, we are prone to the 'correspondence bias', or 'fundamental attribution error'. This is a tendency to overestimate the degree to which people's behaviour is due to their own character traits and intrinsic dispositions, whilst underestimating the degree to which people's behaviour is due to contingent features of the situation they find themselves in. If you see a couple shouting angrily at each other on the street, do you assume that they must be quick-tempered and unstable, or do you assume that they are suffering a life-changing crisis? If a shop manager is effectively directing the work of assistants, do you see this as her natural assertiveness, or as just part of what her job requires?

When we see people behaving in apparently trustworthy ways, speaking honestly and keeping their promises, we are likely to conclude that they are fundamentally trustworthy people. Conversely, when we witness deception or failure to follow through on commitments, we are likely to attribute this to a character flaw, to untrustworthiness. This generates the long-term practical consequences of trustworthiness in attracting trust, and untrustworthiness in attracting suspicion.

As with individuals, if institutions want to be trusted – and they very often do – then they need to think about trustworthiness in this richer sense. That is, they need to develop and demonstrate the willingness and ability to live up to the commitments they incur, both by meeting the commitments they unavoidably have, and by being reflective about adopting new commitments. One aspect of appearing trustworthy involves public statements about what it won't be possible to do, or what won't be attempted within a certain time frame. Over-promising can lead to untrustworthy behaviour, just as easily as bad will or incompetence.

The importance of being trustworthy is central to many areas of life. This means that if we care about fairness, and opportunities for all, we should care about ensuring that everyone has the opportunity to develop and demonstrate trustworthiness. Making commitments, and following through on them, can incur a significant personal cost. And this cost can be especially high for those who already have relatively little material, social, or informational capital. It's easier to be honest about your taxes if you can afford to pay the subsequent bill, it's easier to turn up for appointments on time if you have access to reliable transport, and it's easier to understand the consequences of signing contracts, accepting offers, or taking on responsibilities if you have friends to lean on for advice, and information readily available to you.

The correspondence bias means we underestimate the extent to which we are all influenced by our situations, for better or for worse. So the consequences of being in a difficult situation can be multiplied: if you're going through hard times, it may be more difficult to meet your commitments, and it will be difficult for others to recognize your difficulty, rather than simply writing you off as fecklessly untrustworthy. Judgements about trustworthiness must be handled with care.

Further reading

General overviews

Russell Hardin's introductory *Trust* (Polity Press, 2006) is oriented towards politics and the social sciences; his *Trust and Trustworthiness* (Russell Sage Foundation, 2002) is a lengthier study. Marek Kohn's *Trust: Self Interest and the Common Good* (Oxford University Press, 2008) is a more personal investigation of trust in private and public life. *Building Trust: In Business, Politics, Relationships and Life* (Oxford University Press, 2001) is co-authored by philosopher Robert C. Solomon with Fernando Flores, Chile's finance minister under Allende, later an entrepreneur and consultant in the United States. Together they explore trusting relationships against a business/management backdrop.

Chapter 1: What are trust and distrust?

The open-access online *Stanford Encyclopedia of Philosophy* includes 'Trust', where Carolyn McLeod both reviews philosophical approaches and lists further reading; the same *Encyclopedia* includes 'Pascal's Wager' by Alan Hájek. The essays in *Distrust*, edited by Russell Hardin (Russell Sage Foundation, 2004), examine distrust in its own right.

Chapter 2: Why trust and trustworthiness matter

Onora O'Neill's BBC Reith lectures are published as *A Question of Trust* (Cambridge University Press, 2002). Bruno S. Frey's paper is 'Does Monitoring Increase Work Effort? The Rivalry with Trust and Loyalty', *Economic Inquiry* XXXI (1993). Dyer and Chu's study appears in *Organizational Trust: A Reader*, edited by Roderick M. Kramer (Oxford University Press, 2006); Kramer's collection is a useful resource for students of management.

Chapter 3: Evolving trust and cooperation

Many relevant papers are reprinted in *Trust and Reciprocity* (Russell Sage Foundation, 2003), edited by Elinor Ostrom and James Walker. Text and video for Ostrom's Nobel lecture can be found at www. nobelprize.org. Axelrod and Hamilton's paper is 'The Evolution of Cooperation', *Science* (1981), whilst Cosmides and Tooby's is 'Cognitive Adaptations for Social Exchange', in *The Adapted Mind*, edited by Barkow, Cosmides, and Tooby (Oxford University Press, 1992). *Sense and Nonsense: Evolutionary Perspectives on Human Behaviour*, by Kevin N. Laland and Gillian R. Brown (Cambridge University Press, 2002), clearly reviews issues of kin selection, reciprocal altruism, and cheater detection, whilst *Human Nature after Darwin: A Philosophical Introduction*, by Janet Radcliffe Richards (Routledge, 2000), explores the connections (or lack of them) between biology and morality. *Darwin*, by Tim Lewens (Routledge, 2007), provides helpful context.

Chapter 4: Take the money and run

Trust and Reciprocity, edited by Ostrom and Walker, contains papers relevant to this chapter, as well as to Chapter 3. Ken Binmore's *Game Theory: A Very Short Introduction* (Oxford University Press, 2007) has a chapter on reciprocity. Work on oxytocin is reviewed by Bartz, Zaki, Bolger, and Ochsner in 'Social Effects of Oxytocin in Humans: Context and Person Matter', *Trends in Cognitive Science*, 15(7) (2011). Robert Putnam's *Bowling Alone* (Simon and Schuster, 2000) examines long-term trends in social capital and community. Joseph Henrich and his co-authors summarize their studies of non-industrialized societies in 'In Search of *Homo Economicus*: Behavioral Experiments in 15 Small-Scale Societies', *American Economic Association Papers and Proceedings* (2001).

Chapter 5: Honesty and dishonesty

Ian Leslie's *Born Liars: Why We Can't Live without Deceit* (Quercus, 2011) accessibly explores these issues, and lists further reading. Paul

Ekman's *Telling Lies* (Norton, 2002) sets out his own approach. Darling and Dowdy's research on mothers and adolescents is reported in *Interpersonal Trust during Childhood and Adolescence*, edited by Ken J. Rotenberg (Cambridge University Press, 2010), as is Sakai's research on twins and other siblings. *Testimony: A Philosophical Study*, by C. A. J. Coady (Clarendon, 1992) discusses Hume and Reid, whilst Sperber and co-authors draw together several disciplinary approaches in 'Epistemic Vigilance', *Mind and Language* 25(4) (2010). Jonardon Ganeri's *Philosophy in Classical India* (Routledge, 2001) provides a way into Nyāya thought. Steven Shapin's *A Social History of Truth* (Chicago University Press, 1994) investigates gentlemanly honour. Sarah Stroud's paper is 'Epistemic Partiality in Friendship', *Ethics* 116 (2006); her video discussion with Simon Keller appears on the Philosophy TV website (www. philostv. com).

Chapter 6: Knowledge and expertise

Rethinking Expertise, by Harry Collins and Robert Evans (Chicago University Press, 2007), examines public trust and expertise in science and technology. *Self-Trust and Reproductive Autonomy*, by Carolyn McLeod (MIT Press, 2002), puts self-trust at the heart of ethical issues about reproductive medicine. Miranda Fricker's *Epistemic Injustice* (Oxford University Press, 2007) explores the politics and prejudice which can affect our decisions about trust.

Chapter 7: Trust on the internet

Truth, Lies and Trust on the internet, by Monica T. Whitty and Adam N. Joinson (Routledge, 2009), covers many relevant topics, drawing primarily on psychological research. The philosophy journal *Episteme* devoted its February 2009 issue to questions about knowledge, trust, and Wikipedia.

Chapter 8: Institutions, conspiracies, and nations

Trust within and between Organizations, edited by Christel Lane and Reinhard Bachmann (Oxford University Press, 1998), is a business-oriented collection of papers. Onora O'Neill's *A Question of Trust* (Cambridge University Press, 2002) explores trust in institutions and professions. *Trust and Mistrust in International*

Relations, by Andrew H. Kydd (Princeton University Press, 2005), discusses trust and cooperation, especially surrounding the Cold War. *Conspiracy Theories: The Philosophical Debate*, edited by David Coady (Ashgate, 2006), is a relatively sober collection of papers that includes a reprint of Brian Keeley's essay.

Index

Index

Index

Expand your collection of
VERY SHORT INTRODUCTIONS

FREE WILL

A Very Short Introduction
Thomas Pink

Every day we seem to make and act upon all kinds of free choices—some trivial, and others so consequential that they may change the course of our life. But are these choices really free? Or are we compelled to act the way we do by factors beyond our control? Is the feeling that we could have made different decisions just an illusion? And if our choices are not free, is it legitimate to hold people morally responsible for their actions?

This Very Short introduction looks at a range of issues surrounding this fundamental philosophical question. Exploring free will through the ideas of the Greek and medieval philosophers up to present-day thinkers, Thomas Pink provides an original and incisive introduction to this perennially fascinating subject, and a new defence of the reality of human free will.

www.oup.com/vsi

THE MEANING OF LIFE
A Very Short Introduction
Terry Eagleton

'Philosophers have an infuriating habit of analysing questions rather than answering them', writes Terry Eagleton, who, in these pages, asks the most important question any of us ever ask, and attempts to answer it. So what is the meaning of life? In this witty, spirited, and stimulating inquiry, Eagleton shows how centuries of thinkers - from Shakespeare and Schopenhauer to Marx, Sartre and Beckett - have tackled the question. Refusing to settle for the bland and boring, Eagleton reveals with a mixture of humour and intellectual rigour how the question has become particularly problematic in modern times. Instead of addressing it head-on, we take refuge from the feelings of 'meaninglessness' in our lives by filling them with a multitude of different things: from football and sex, to New Age religions and fundamentalism.

'Light hearted but never flippant.'

The Guardian.